COVID CHRONICLES

College Students Navigate Pandemic Life

Compiled by Professor David Blow

Outskirts Press, Inc.
http://www.outskirtspress.com

ISBN: 978-1-9772-3915-0

Cover Photo © 2021 David Blow. All rights reserved - used with permission.
Front Cover Design by Jasmin Gomez and Anthony Richichi, Back Cover Design by Rhonda Triller.

Outskirts Press and the "OP" logo are trademarks belonging to Outskirts Press, Inc.

PRINTED IN THE UNITED STATES OF AMERICA

Dedication

This book is dedicated to the Castleton University students in my Fall 2020 Media Writing class who authored the words you're about to read. Despite the hardships of trying to learn online during a pandemic, they excelled and inspired me to compile their work and share it with the world.

Life is tough for everyone during this pandemic, but college students are losing so much of that sacred experience and my goal through this project was to provide them with a needed win.

I hope this book accomplishes that in some way.

Special thanks to Jasmin Gomez and Anthony Richichi for their work on the cover and to editor Rhonda Triller, who also designed the back jacket.

Table of Contents

Foreword

TEACHING COLLEGE STUDENTS online during a pandemic isn't easy. As a 53-year-old professor who hates sitting, gets bulging eyes when I speak and loves to bounce around the classroom pulling answers out of students, the Brady Bunch-esque Zoom screen just doesn't cut it for me – or them.

So I tried to think of different ideas to engage students and let them vent about this college experience-robbing pandemic.

Enter what I called "COVID Chronicles," a biweekly blog in my Media Writing class that became a bonanza of amazing, emotional, raw content – ranging from thankfulness for unplanned family time to fear of losing loved ones. One student, a Vermonter born in Korea and adopted by a seventh-generation Vermont family, wrote about feeling staring, blaming eyes on her now.

Every other week, a new batch of struggles, triumphs and anecdotes appeared in the assignment discussion board. I read them, one by one, and learned about their upside-down lives in relative isolation.

One day, I thought, these blogs really represent a valuable snapshot in history with a worldwide pandemic unseen in 100 years.

And, I thought, "They belong in a book."

My students can be the face of an anywhere-in-the-country university in 2020.

They're at Castleton University in Vermont, but their fears and hopes are universal.

I pitched the idea and they all quickly agreed to let their work be used.

But before I let you get to their work, I want to try to convey what these students have done for me this semester.

I went from panicked dad in March, trying desperately to get my two daughters home from Europe just as the continent was closing down, to thankful dad riding out a pandemic as a crazy family of four. There were intense and scary COVID-related mental health issues in the summer, but also lots of laughter and thankful times.

As fall semester approached, I knew the university was offering online-only classes and I prepared hard for it. But honestly, I dreaded the unknown. I LOVE the classroom and love when students pop into to my office for help or just to chat.

That wasn't happening this semester, for the first time in my 15 years as a full-time professor.

But from the start, this Media Writing class lifted my spirits.

They seemed to eagerly tackle everything I threw at them -- from press releases and screenplays to radio ads and public service announcements.

In these blogs, however, they offered up large pieces of themselves for me and their classmates to read. I found myself saddened one minute by the mental health issues and hopelessness and then laughing or smiling at their wit, and admiring their compassion and wisdom.

They interacted with each other on their posts too, sometimes commiserating, sometimes trying to help with thoughtful words.

I was so grateful for what they were giving me through their writing, I felt compelled to thank them. This was my email to the class:

Hi guys,

So it's 8:28 on a Saturday morning and I'm grading stuff - before going to the dump, doing laundry, walking the dog etc. before hopefully hitting a golf ball or playing pickleball or rollerblading later. (Glamorous prof. life, right?)

But I just felt compelled to say thanks for the effort on these blogs. As I type this, I honestly have tears in my eyes from what I'm reading. Not sad tears because they're awful, or because of what the virus is doing messing with our lives, but happy tears at the amazing, clever writing, the sharing of personal stories of hardships and triumphs and thankfulness and anger and wishfulness ... I'm blown away and I tell anybody who asks "how's all-online teaching going?" that you guys are lifting me up and inspiring me with the power of your words and how you're putting them together.

So, thanks!

Dave

I hope their words make you think, make you laugh or smile or ponder your own situation. And I hope they offer a true glimpse of their chaotic pandemic lives, and how despite missing out on so much that we have long taken for granted, they are powering through.

Professors are supposed to inspire students, and I hope I do that frequently. But in the crazy Fall 2020 semester, these students inspired me.

CHAPTER 1

Lily Doton

Lily Doton's first blog in this series was a major spark for the idea to publish "COVID Chronicles" into a book. As an Asian Vermonter, she has a very different take on COVID-19 and the blame game that ensued. Her subsequent entries were equally powerful and well-written, detailing the dog days of the pandemic.

Now they don't ask

As funny as it may sound, I haven't always known that I'm not white.

When I was a kid, I thought that me and my definitely nonbiological, white brother were twins. We had the same color hair and the same color eyes. What more did we need to fit the criteria?

As I got older, my pin-straight black hair and the shape of my eyes stood out to me more and more. These features provided onlookers with a perception of me that I had no say in. This is more apparent to me now more than ever.

When COVID-19 hit the world, so did a rise in casual racism against East Asian people. I can't count the number of bat-eating jokes I've seen online, exacerbated by Donald Trump referring to the coronavirus as the "Chinese virus."

I began to see videos of Asian people getting assaulted and verbally attacked, restaurants losing business and personal accounts of the discomfort many Asian Americans experienced during this time.

I have always felt relatively sheltered from this kind of violence in Vermont, but the unease has sat with me since late March.

Maybe it's just my paranoia, but I swear I can feel everyone's eyes on me, watching me warily as I walk into the grocery store fully masked. As if I pose more of a threat than the white people coming up to Vermont from New York, Connecticut, Massachusetts.

The question "Where are you from?" has always held a lot of weight for people of color, but I find myself wishing they'd choose to ask it now. Let me explain that I've lived in Vermont for 21 years. Maybe if I get the chance, I can tell them I was adopted by a family of seventh-generation Vermonters when I was a baby, and the tension will dissipate.

But this is one of the times when they don't ask.

A derailed new start

COVID-19 has been lonely.

Prior to the pandemic, after about a year off from school, I decided I was ready to apply to transfer and return to student life. I officially sent in my application to Castleton in April, back when I was sure the pandemic wouldn't last through the summer.

To be honest, I enjoyed the first few months. My job was shut down so I had all the free time in the world, and all of my friends were coming back from school after months of me being alone in my hometown.

But then it dragged on. And on. And on.

I couldn't see my friends all the time, even though they were so close now. I couldn't see a future where I'd be able to freely hug them again, instead of making sure we're keeping our distance.

I got my Castleton acceptance letter, and the thought of my own space, new friends and interesting classes kept me going. I signed a lease on an apartment and started thinking about the decoration possibilities.

Soon after, I found out that all classes would be online.

Part of me expected this; it was the safest decision for students, professors and all our families.

But I was still disappointed. On one hand, it would help me ease back into school. On the other, I would likely be in my apartment alone all the time.

Both are true now.

I'm an introvert and I love alone time, but not when alone time is literally all the time.

The tiny bit of social interaction I get every day is through a screen, staring at the boxes displaying my classmates' faces, none of whom I've ever met in person.

Making friends in online classes feels almost impossible.

There are days when it doesn't affect me at all, when I feel good about where I am.

But there are also days when it creeps in, when I'm scrolling through old pictures on my phone and the loneliness takes over.

He's the light

At 12:45 a.m. on Oct. 1, my older sister finally had her baby.

When I woke up and saw the texts, a sense of relief rushed through my body. Everything went well.

It has been scary to see her pregnant during a global pandemic, and I've been at least a little bit on edge about it every day since COVID grew worse. We're in a fairly safe state, but the anxiety over it would not go away.

When my oldest brother and his wife had their first baby, I was able to rush to Connecticut and see him in the hospital. That wasn't possible this time – my sister's husband was the only one allowed in the room with her.

But baby Benen is finally here, and everyone is safe.

Benen is an Irish name that means "kind and benevolent" and I can already tell that it's perfect for him.

My sister Annie and I got the chance to FaceTime this afternoon so she could show me his tiny, sleepy face. As soon as we hung up, I burst into tears.

Tears of joy, excitement, relief.

I could tell she was tired, but so, so happy.

I'm not sure when I'll be able to hold him, unmasked, and freely kiss his forehead, but any disappointment I may have over that is washed away when I look at the pictures Annie has sent me.

In a time that has been extremely dark, it feels like he is the light.

Lost time

I think back to March, April, May, June, and I genuinely can't remember what I did. Here are some of the things I *do* remember:

1. Staring at the wall and having an existential crisis. I know I definitely did this (at least) weekly.
2. Planning a FaceTime with my friends. And then never actually calling my friends. I don't know why; it's not that we were too busy.
3. Going through my old bookshelf. Finding a "Twilight" book and reading the entire series cover to cover over the course of three days. Feeling immediate shame for spending my time reading "Twilight" of all things.
4. Scrolling through Twitter. Endlessly.
5. Forgetting to text all my friends back.
6. Getting caught up reading the news – COVID, Donald Trump, BLM – spiraling myself into a mini anxiety attack.
7. Pulling an all-nighter doing absolutely nothing. But who cares? I have no reason to get up and be productive tomorrow.
8. Watching all my old videos from the BTS concert I went to last year. Blankly staring at the tickets I had bought for this year. Maybe I cried (I definitely did; don't make fun of me).

9. Online shopping for hours and buying things I didn't need to fill the void.
10. Going to the grocery store. Panicking the entire time I'm there, and wiping down everything with hydrogen peroxide when I got home.
11. Spending a whole day watching an entire series of a show I don't even remember the details of now.
12. More scrolling through Twitter, more staring at the wall.

And through all this, life went on. I spent months doing nothing, but time refused to stop. Now things are going back to "normal" and I can't remember what it was like before.

Some of the people I know are back to trying to live the way they were pre-COVID, some are still cooped up in their houses, and some of them I haven't talked to since March.

So what now?

It shouldn't all fall on us, but ...

Ask anyone, and I'm sure they would say that we're living in "unprecedented times."

It sounds exciting, right?

It's not.

Personally, I'm really, really sick of it.

We're in the middle of a global pandemic, the likes of which hasn't been seen since 1918. For the first time ever, almost everyone has to learn solely through a screen.

Our president is a privileged businessman turned reality TV star turned, well, "commander in chief," who is attempting to stop votes from being counted because they aren't in his favor.

On that topic, our current choices for president are either old white guy I don't like or old white guy I loathe. Scientists have said that we have maybe about 10 years left to combat climate change before the damage is irreversible, yet half our citizens (including half of our policy makers) don't even believe that climate change exists.

"Black lives matter" (simply matter) is one of the most controversial things you can say. In 2020.

Political parties are more polarized than ever and it doesn't feel completely ridiculous to think a second civil war could be brewing.

On one hand, I really think we're screwed.

On the other, I have at least some hope for the future. I know so many people my age who are incredibly passionate about changing the country and even the world.

In some ways, these "unprecedented times" have been really inspiring. Seeing Black Lives Matter protests in all 50 states for months, some even until now, inspired me.

Watching people my age and younger speaking out about politics and urging people to vote inspired me.

Our generation has incredibly high depression and anxiety rates, maybe due in part to mental health becoming slightly less stigmatized and more people being open to talking about it.

Maybe because this is the world we're inheriting.

But I think if any generation can solve these problems, it will be ours (even if it would be cool if the responsibility didn't completely fall on us ... we'll see).

CHAPTER 2

Mason Svayg

The class grew to depend on Mason to elevate the mood during COVID Chronicles blog discussion days. His posts were cheery, very observant and often both thankful and reflective. He spoke repeatedly about being lucky for his secluded mountaintop surroundings while the world was being devastated by the disease.

COVID created stronger family bond

This pandemic really threw me off. I imagine it did for everyone else also.

Even though life is different now, it's still a wonderful world. Yes, we may have to wear masks, we can't party anymore, no more taking road trips from state to state, no more sharing each other's drinks – and lots of hand sanitizer.

But even though this is the new norm, make the best out of it, because sadly nothing is going to change for at least another year. The norm now will continue to be the norm for the many months to come.

Look outside: There's so much to do.

Mother Nature is beautiful and it's where I have spent most of my time during COVID. It's peaceful. You'll hear birds singing, crickets chirping. Take a walk, look at the clouds, look at the trees. Be grateful for what you see.

Along with soaking up the sunshine, family has been everything. Spending time with my family over these past six months has really been great. It made me realize how much I missed my family while away at college. Every day I am surrounded by my mom, my dad, brother, sister and three dogs. As each day goes by, our family bond grows stronger. We listen to my dad's old cassette tapes, laugh and play board games, and every Sunday night we make sushi for dinner.

COVID really hasn't impacted my life in a bad way. I still strive to be grateful for what I have and, of course, make the best out of every situation.

So, listen to some Jack Johnson, make some art, maybe inhale a little green and everything will be just fine. Our world is still spinning with laughter and joy.

I wish they could see what I see

As we look outside, we see a beautiful state.

But as we look outside this beautiful state, we see death, along with sadness and grief for those who have lost their lives due to this terrible sickness.

I wish people could see what I see every day when I wake up.

The sun rising, telling life to wake up.

Birds are singing to the new light.

My little sister is running in circles around the house, chasing our newest member of the family, Luna the puppy.

As I walk down the stairs every morning, I go to the kitchen. I start by making a cup of coffee, black as always, along with either a bagel or blueberry pancakes.

I then go outside and say good morning to my best friend Niles, the adventurous dog.

He wags his tail as he jumps up and down. He knows I'm about to greet him with the new day.

I now begin homework in the room we call the greenhouse. It has 10 huge windows and a clear roof above.

As I look outside the many windows, I see leaves starting to change color. Winter is coming.

We had our first fire of the year last night as it dropped below freezing here in the north.

I question if this winter will bring more and more death as temps drop, and green slowly fades to brown, with snow all over.

I spend most of my time in the greenhouse room, thinking about shit I've never thought of before in between Zoom class calls.

My mind wanders, just like this virus, affecting people as it leaves a trail of death.

I think about life, love, past experiences that brought forth thrill, and last, family, and friends.

But, I do wonder what those 929,000 people thought of before passing away due to COVID-19.

Was it love?

Was it past experiences that brought forth thrill, or laughter?

Was it friends, and family?

Or was it everything?

I truly wish those 929,000 people could see what I see.

Waking up in the morning, alive.

Opa's vinyl collection is pandemic panacea

Here I am, surrounded by vinyl.

In the middle, I sit on the comfiest one-seater couch.

I've just received roughly 300 records from my Opa's entire old collection. Ever since I laid my hands on these records, I've listened to new ones every day.

It took me a while, but all 300-plus records are now alphabetized by band names. The majority of my free time is now spent listening to these records.

I've learned a lot by listening to these beautiful vinyls.

It's crucial to listen to the whole album – side one and two.

Every album tells a story.

Every album is different, and every album has a different personality, much like a book.

I've only listened to about 25 so far. If you think about it, I could almost listen to a new record every day of the year.

Name a band from the '60s through the '90s and I probably have at least one of their albums.

Of the 300-plus records that were gifted to me, I don't even know half of the bands.

I have a lot of listening to do, and learning.

Since the vast spread of the virus, life hasn't brought forth much worry, or fear.

I am lucky where I live, in the middle of nowhere.

Life has been pretty good, and now with these vinyls, it's even better.

Music is wonderful; it brings people and cultures together.

It puts smiles on people's faces.

Maybe our world needs to listen to more music. We are sadly more divided now than ever.

Shout out to Media Writing class

Coming into this semester, I was very skeptical about taking all online classes.

After the first couple of weeks went by though, it wasn't so bad. I got the work done, but I kinda just got it done to get it done.

Being all online is harder to want to learn, rather than being in a classroom where you are more focused and are actually intrigued to want to learn.

I will say, Media Writing with you, Dave Blow, is the only class where I feel intrigued and actually look forward to Zoom class calls.

You bring the energy with you anywhere you go. Other than this class, I literally just get the work done to get it done.

I'm sorry, but I'm starting to get really sick of all my other classes. Like Critical Thinking, holy shit do you have to think. It's so much goddamn thinking.

I am very much looking forward to this two-month break ahead of us. I really need that shit. I can finally not think about school, and just vibe, do whatever comes to my mind.

Go snowboarding, drink midweek, stay up late, roll as many doobies as I want, and again, just vibe.

Maybe I'll even make some music. Who knows? All I do know is I have two months to finally chill, and do what I want to do.

CHAPTER 3

Rielly Johnson

Rielly's post about his grandmother contracting COVID-19 brought a new reality to the class and to the assignment. Rielly also brought a conversational writing style that made you feel his fear of the disease in a subsequent post.

When COVID hit home

Waking up the day the pandemic started was like waking up in an alternate dimension. You see movies and read history books about past pandemics, but they've always just been exactly that: history.

No one I know was expecting COVID-19 to have the effect it did, and no one expected they would ever be able to catch it. For a while, it was hard to even grasp that it was real and actually happening.

Quarantine was difficult, and the masks were annoying at first, but it wasn't until June 13 that my family really had to face COVID-19.

My grandmother called my mom that morning to announce she had tested positive for coronavirus. I first remember the feeling in my chest, like something was holding onto me and squeezing just enough to make it harder to breathe, but not enough to take my breath away entirely.

I had seen the news. I had read all the articles: COVID-19 affected the elderly far worse than it would affect me. It was natural for me to start thinking of the worst possible outcomes when the world was losing its collective mind over this.

For days, it was a waiting game. She'd been quarantined at her local hospital, and we were unable to see her for a long time, which made the waiting all that much more unbearable.

My extended family gathered together for group calls a few times, just to talk and distract ourselves from the heaping amount of worry we felt for my grandmother. A week or so later, we received another call from her.

My grandmother sounded ecstatic.

The virus has passed, and she was OK.

I let out a breath of relief I realize I'd been holding back since the phone rang. Although I had initially thought I was looking at one of the hardest times in my life, my grandmother made a steady recovery and the experience gave me a reality check about how important wearing a mask is, and how important it is to self-distance whenever and wherever you can.

As if moving isn't bad enough without COVID-19

One of the most stressful things a person can willingly do is move houses.

There's just so much that goes into it: packing, unpacking, checking and double-checking to be sure you didn't miss anything, still thinking you forgot something despite even triple-checking before you left your old house, then settling into your new place in hopes that it will start to feel like home.

I've moved twice this year.

It's no secret that COVID-19 has increasingly made even the simplest of tasks just a little bit harder than they were before. Unfortunately for me, adding a pandemic to what was already a notoriously stressful situation made everything that much more difficult.

When I received the news campus was shutting down, my mom

insisted that I come home right away, but was in no position to be able to come pick me up.

I don't have my own car and my friends all live about two hours away from me, so I was left with one option: the bus.

People who know me know I have a lot of things. I had two suit-cases full of clothes, two backpacks, another suitcase with miscel-laneous things from around my room I couldn't get rid of, all things I had to carry onto this bus, and keep track of in order to keep from losing it all.

I eventually made it home, got help carrying all my things to the car, and everything made it back to my mom's place safely. I man-aged to unpack it all over the course of a few weeks and, by June, I felt comfortable enough to call the space I'm staying in "my room."

Two months later, I'm packing it all up again.

There's more excitement this time, since I'm moving to an apart-ment I can call my own, but the stress is still there, unsettling.

I don't ride the bus this time. And over the summer, I somehow managed to collect more things that I really don't need, but I get a ride from a friend who empathizes with the way moving during COVID can give you a different, special kind of worry.

I'm still unpacking and settling in, but the stress of moving dimin-ishes just a little bit more each day.

Do I have it?

There's a lot of paranoia circling around.

I've always been quick to worry, but it has become increasingly hard to relax this year due to news, skepticism, quarantine, etc.

The other day, I woke up with a sore throat and panic quickly settled in. I've looked up symptoms of coronavirus multiple times, but I had to look them up again just to unnecessarily remind myself that a sore throat was, in fact, one of the symptoms.

So, I was left between telling myself I somehow contracted COVID and in the same breath, telling myself that I don't have nearly enough symptoms. I continued jumping back and forth through different websites to check and double check if there's anything I'm missing.

Eventually I had to laugh, because I know I wasn't even acting like myself anymore. I'm panicking over something I could have easily gotten checked, and it would have confirmed whether I had corona or not. I called around and quickly found a place willing to give me a test the same day, and the next day, I got negative results.

But my sore throat has gotten worse and I've read about coronavirus tests being wrong sometimes. The worry still settles in the back of my mind as I try my best to ignore it.

I've been tested, I've done research, and all I'm able to do now is wait. Logically, I think I'd be feeling much worse if I had corona, but it's completely out of my control now and I think that's the scariest part.

Pandemic brings ADHD more into focus

I've always known there was something that made it a bit difficult to cope with learning and being in a classroom environment.

From the very first time I sat down at a desk, opened my notebook and looked up at my first-grade teacher, I found it increasingly hard to focus on what was happening in front of me.

I looked around, hoping to find someone looking back at me, but there was no one I could find to make eye contact with. All the other students were looking at the teacher, something I should have been able to do.

I tried, for a while.

I tried to stare at the teacher's face, or at the board, and then there'd be a pink marker just out of my peripheral vision, or someone walking by the window directly to my left and, for some reason, that was far more interesting to me than anything my teacher had to say.

When I was 10, I was diagnosed with ADHD. I had no idea what it meant at the time. As it was described to me, I was under the impression that I'd just be a little distracted or hyperactive. I figured it was something I could handle.

So did my dad, apparently, because he turned down any offers for a prescription. Elementary school was a vicious cycle of testing outside of my grade level and then being put in advanced classes I would have to be removed from halfway through the school year because I couldn't focus long enough to get any work done.

The education system just didn't cater to me. It never would. For the better part of my life, ADHD just meant I was easily distracted. It took me 10 years to realize how wrong I was.

Still untracked, my ADHD has become one of my biggest roadblocks in life. With online classes in full swing this year, I had to rely entirely on myself to get my work done in a timely manner and it created one of the most difficult years of my life.

Not only did it affect me academically, but mentally as well. With the pressure of school, work and everything else in my life, I found it incredibly taxing to cope with COVID on top of all that.

It wasn't until this year that I did my own research on the effects of ADHD and it's a whole lot more than just being easily distracted. Sleep disturbance, forgetfulness, poor sense of time and several learning disabilities I never understood were caused by my ADHD.

These are things that were never addressed by any of the adults in my life growing up. I'd been to several school counselors, had several teachers, and none of them thought to have a talk with me about why I was having such a hard time being "normal."

I don't think any of them really understood the full meaning of ADHD, either. I've recently had it described to me as an iceberg. Above the water, the hyperactivity and the inability to focus are all recognized symptoms. But all the other possible effects it has often go ignored. This makes it incredibly hard for kids with ADHD to cope, especially with school, since without access to proper help, they're almost doomed to fail.

Facing worldwide challenges such as the pandemic is hard enough as it is, but for neurodivergent people it has that effect tenfold, especially when it's left unmedicated or unaccommodated, because they already face day-to-day challenges.

Realizing the different effects of having ADHD and how it has affected me personally has been the first step in finding ways to cope with it and help make my life less complicated. Although this year has been especially demanding, it also gave me a reason to start looking into ways I can help myself and maybe even help others who have had similar experiences with learning disabilities as I have along the way.

CHAPTER 4

Aurora Calchera (and then Aurora Calchera-Champine)

Aurora tells herself she's a graphic designer and artist – and she is. Without prompting, she created a mock cover for this book. But she is also a powerful writer and quickly became a class favorite with her cleverly written COVID tales. Oh, and she also got married mid-semester, mid-pandemic!

Not how it was supposed to go

The Year of the Rat was supposed to be my year.

Around mid-November of 2019, I exited a four-year-long depression. The realization came to me softly, subtly, quietly – and not long after, it was gone. I can't explain it: Just that *it* wasn't there anymore. Like the moment you're feeling your way out of a fog and you suddenly touch clear air.

Maybe I was lucky?

But I'm never lucky.

With the flood gates open and the serotonin flowing, I envisioned all the accomplishments I wanted to achieve, and I attacked them in a fervor state of productivity because I knew at any time *it* could come back without knocking.

I created a draft for success to help me navigate all the complexities of my personal projects, the tedium of finishing my last year as an academic and the ambitions of a fulfilling professional career.

I thought it was perfect.

For the first time, I said, "I can do this."

Cut to two months later, New Year's Eve, and I was about to start 2020 perfectly – by going to bed early. It may not seem important, but in my mind, starting out the year with a healthy, controlled habit contributed to the foundation I was determined to build my success on.

Year of the Rat, bring it on!

I also hate loud noises and I hate that moment when the ball drops and everyone loses their minds.

I believe my exact words were: "F*ck that."

It is now early September.

Am I where I want to be?

No.

Am I wiser for it?

Sure.

But I take back what I said earlier about not being lucky: I AM lucky. My lungs breathe on their own and I haven't had to attend a funeral through a Zoom call.

Do I want things to go back to the way they were?

Never!

A different kind of overwhelming

I thought the routine would be good for me, but now it's suffocating.

My only relief from the confines of my apartment are at the gym in the morning, and the odd errand or appointment later in the day. If I'm lucky.

The rest of the time is spent shifting from the bed to the couch to my desk, and then back to the couch but maybe back to my desk later.

After about three hours of procrastinating, I take a break to make tea in the tiny little kitchen and then go right back to avoiding the grind. 2020 goals.

I live in a complex with about five or six other apartments in the building, so space outside isn't abundant nor private. I wouldn't recommend going for a walk on Route 4 since the shoulders are narrow and people either drive way too slow or way too fast. You don't want to be on the blind corner either way.

School has taken on a new definition of tedium. I took being on campus for granted for sure. I forgot how much I rely on face-to-face communication to learn, especially with difficult subjects. Plus having that connection with other classmates is invaluable.

But for as much as I can complain, it's not all bad. I'm productive in a lot of other ways, especially creatively. Too many ideas are just bursting at the seams. I need to keep reminding myself that this whole experience is just a different kind of overwhelming that I'm not used to.

Pandemic wedding planning

Planning a wedding is stressful, but planning a wedding in the middle of a pandemic is stressful stress that has been drenched in palpable inconvenience.

If I had it my way, we would have showed up by ourselves on a weekday at a courthouse to have a judge, whom neither of us have ever met nor would meet again, tell us, through a mask, while reading text from a piece of printer copy paper that we were now legally responsible for each other until we either decide to call it quits or until we die, whichever came first.

Needless to say, that idea was nixed real quick.

Instead, the future Mr. and I found middle ground, not in the lobby of a government building, but in the foyer of a castle.

The Wilson Castle is a lovely piece of history just outside of downtown Rutland, Vermont in beautiful Proctor. Somehow, we agreed that it's a favorite place for both of us, despite having never been inside the place together up until two days ago.

Eight Amazon packages, five phone calls, three exchanges, two returns, one argument and one mental breakdown later, a wedding plan was made in just under five weeks (knock on wood).

So far, I would say the biggest problems came when organizing the guest list. Due to the pandemic, it was impossible for it to be a big party; I had heard horror stories about such things on the news.

It ultimately meant that most of my extended family wouldn't be able to attend since they live in Massachusetts, a necessary but potentially lifesaving sacrifice. After a month of deliberation, we presented the list to the families on a strict need-to-know-basis.

It's amazing how two families can hear the words, "I want to make this as simple as possible," and proceed to make every minute detail as unnecessarily complex as possible.

There were several times I was starting to miss my courthouse idea.

Yet after the dust settled and the logistics were finalized, I think everyone is just excited now.

I've been overwhelmed by the love, support and respect we've received. I've heard other people who are engaged say it's pointless to get married this year. And maybe they're right.

But if this pandemic has shown me anything, it's that if you have any opportunity to make your own happiness, you should take it because something as simple as the next 12 hours are never guaranteed.

Media Writing class a pandemic positive

A blank screen holds many possibilities. But a blank mind is like a Pythagorean Cup and ideas are the wine: too much of a good thing and it starts leaking out.

What's there to write about that hasn't already been written? I'm trying to piece together thoughts like cuts of fabric for a quilt to form a cohesive experience, but nothing looks right stitched to another.

How many different ways can I say I'm emotionally tired?

How can I put into words the deep loneliness I feel when I look at a Zoom class and there are all black screens? How many questions do I have to ask before I get answers?

Maybe it's because I lack purpose in all this. I'm not on the front lines of anything. I'm just a quiet supporter in the back, not making the problems worse but not actively making things better.

I'm not making amazing art or authoring compelling stories to ease the eyes and minds of an audience. And I can't keep writing the same email, week after week, to my professors that says sorry I'm behind on everything even when I have no excuse, except that I have an all-season pass with the Struggle Bus.

Sometimes being too good with words can mean too much thought and less action.

But that's enough with that.

Ain't no rest for the wicked, or so they say.

Let's end this with a good note: I want to say thank you to all of my professors this semester, especially to Bill DeForest and David Blow – Bill, for your unending support for almost three years, and David for having us write these blogs.

As much of a pain as they are, they've also been the most re-warding assignment. Thank you to all the professors and faculty at Castleton University, who keep going every day despite the wall of black screens. I know that's probably not what you signed up for.

To my classmates in Media Writing, our class has been the ab-solute highlight of the year because of you guys. Lastly, thank you to every health care worker in our community, for your dedication and perseverance even when the odds are against you. I definitely know this isn't something you signed up for.

CHAPTER 5

Jacob Gonzalez

Jacob is a big, burly football player who opened up to the class through these blogs about what the coronavirus did to his already-fragile mental state. One of the most positive moments to come out of this COVID Chronicles assignment happened during a discussion of that week's entries when he told the class how valuable the assignment was to help his deteriorating mental state. He also often detailed worrying about his mom.

COVID-19, mom and depression

Home in March?

Who would've thought I would be on my way home for the last time during this spring semester? It didn't feel right walking into my house so soon, but I was very happy to see my mom.

My mom is a very important person in my life. When I first left for college, I was very homesick for a lot of reasons, but I was mainly sad about leaving my mom for the first time for such a long time.

My mom and I have a special relationship. She has taken care of me for basically my whole life. You could say I'm a little bit of a mama's boy and I probably wouldn't disagree with you.

Arriving with a big hug and the sensational smell of snickerdoodle cookies, my favorite, I was very happy to be home.

Beep. Beep. Beep.

My mom's insulin pump was going off yet again screaming at her that her sugar was low. As usual, I ran to the end of the hallway to grab her a juice box while she pricked her finger to test her blood.

My mom has been a Type 1 diabetic since she was 7 years old. Throughout the years, she had to deal with the hardships of being a diabetic by sticking a needle in her finger every day, staying on a consistent diet and the worst of all, enduring a weak immune system.

Her weak immune system has put her in the hospital multiple times and it has always been a worry for me. Seeing my own mother being rushed out of the house because of a simple cold has always stuck with me to make sure I'm keeping her safe at any cost.

And coronavirus was another obstacle we had to face.

After studies came out showing that Type 1 diabetics are at high risk of dying when getting the coronavirus, my mom had to be careful. So after only one week of being home, I was officially quarantined since I had to stay inside to protect my mom.

I fully understood why I couldn't go see my friends, but I was the only one out of my friend group who had to be quarantined.

At first, I didn't mind being stuck inside every hour, but soon enough, I started to feel alone. With all this time to myself, I started to become depressed. Overthinking one thing after another, my mind was filled with negative thoughts.

My depression and anxiety had come back yet again, taking over my body in a way I've never experienced before.

Things got dark

Quarantine had officially started.

To keep my mother safe, I had to stay inside and stop hanging out with my friends unless we were socially distant. My friends still continued to hang out every day, but I was prevented from hanging out with them.

So there I was.

Alone.

Stuck in my room.

Wondering when this would end.

For the two months I stayed in my house, I had the same schedule every day.

I would wake up five minutes before my class and try to pay attention to what was going on, trying to get used to class through Zoom and the fact I was still sleeping mentally.

After class, I would do homework for hours because all my professors thought that giving us double the work was a good idea. I would average about six to eight hours a day just doing homework and studying alone. After hours of homework, I went to work out at my friend's gym in his house.

My mom allowed me to go to CJ's house because she knew I needed to work out for football. Each day I had to send in a video of me working out to my coaches to show them I wasn't just sitting around during this time.

I would come home to finish homework or play Xbox until I eventually went to bed.

Every day.

The same exact routine.

After a month, I started to feel alone. I felt hopeless as I reflected on all the things planned for 2020.

There were many nights when I would just think about my future and if I'd be able to make it out of this situation. I started to over-think everything, which triggered my anxiety and filled my mind with negativity.

It got to the point where all my thoughts were only focusing on the negatives in life.

I've been here before.

Depression.

I had nobody but myself to talk about things that were in my head. This only made matters worse. The darkest days of quarantine had taken over my mental state, which caused one of the worst months of my life.

Proving myself wrong

June is the start of summer. June is the transitional period for everyone to finally be free and happy. June is also my birthday month and I was going to celebrate my 19th birthday.

But June 2020 was one of the worst months of my life.

The reason?

Overthinking my purpose in life.

I began to question a lot of things about myself. Is college really the right path to my future? Why am I not where I want to be yet? Am I ever going to make it out of this?

I would dwell on these thoughts night after night. Countless nights I'd get little to no sleep and that became the new norm for me as I tried to figure it out.

It only got worse.

I became less and less productive throughout each day as I'd go to work and come back home to rekindle the thoughts I had the previous night.

It felt like a never-ending black hole that I didn't think I would ever get out of. Talking to people only made things worse for myself as I didn't get the feedback I was looking for.

I was alone.

I had nobody.

I was empty.

Depression isn't new to me. I've been through a lot throughout my life, but this was something I've never experienced. Feeling this hopeless has never happened to me and the thoughts that went through my head are thoughts I never want anyone to experience.

It's truly scary reflecting on these thoughts and what could've happened.

I knew I was stronger than that. The week leading up to my birthday, I took that time to reflect on the things I've yet to achieve in life.

I thought about what it's going to be like when I can finally tell myself, "I made it."

I wanted to prove to myself that I could get through this. I've gotten through so much by myself already, I thought, so why couldn't I do it again?

On my birthday, June 29, I wrote on my white board in big letters, "PROVE YOURSELF WRONG," to remind myself what my purpose is in life.

I've battled with negative thoughts almost every day that I wouldn't make it. Now, I live by this statement to remind myself of how far I've come and what is yet to come in my lifetime.

A semester of growth

Going into the new year, I don't think anyone expected this to happen.

This has been a tough year for all of us as we all struggled and continue to struggle every day.

Getting the news of not playing football in July and not returning to see all my friends at college after leaving months prior really sucked. I wasn't very optimistic going into my sophomore year as I thought this was going to be a very difficult time.

It was definitely made easier as I met my new professors and I started to get back into a schedule. Going to class, going to the gym and hanging out with my friends and family has been my routine since the start of the new semester.

I was thankful to get some really cool professors, who have been very lenient with the situation we are in and that has made things a lot easier compared with the final weeks of the spring semester.

I've learned a lot throughout this semester about myself. I've learned that class through a computer screen is one of the most frustrating things in the world, yet an experience that many people can't say they've had.

I've learned that I can maintain my good work ethic, whether it's at school or in my bed half-awake.

I've also learned that I can get through any obstacles that get thrown at me. Football season being canceled and not being able to reconnect with friends and enjoy the college life is one of the hardest things I've had to overcome.

I can confidently say, however, I have gotten through the toughest year of my life and we only have two months left to the new year as I'm writing this.

As we're closing in on the end of my fall semester, which is crazy to say, we can all finally take these last few weeks to be thankful to not have lost our minds fully. And with that being said, this has been Jacob Gonzalez signing off. One. Final. Time.

CHAPTER 6

Joey Verbaro

Joey was one of the few students in class to live on campus during the fall semester. He wrote about family and friends a lot and documented a COVID scare that forced him into quarantine on campus for a week. As trying as that was, it provided him material for a screenplay assignment that proved to be his crowning achievement in the class, with him offering an emotional, soul-purging acting display portraying himself. After sending students drafts of their chapters to review, Joey's mom, who was help-  *ing with revisions, revealed that he is on the autism spectrum saying, "Joey is a very visual writer, a trait that he learned from living with autism his entire life."*

Feeling troubled, but grateful

During this pandemic, my whole family was scared and weirdly curious how long this would last or if we would get back to some type of normal in this modern world.

It was back in March when I got the email about campus closing for an early spring break and honestly, I was nervous. I was worried about my friends I met on campus last semester and my family at home preparing for the lockdown.

I called my parents Thursday and they picked me up on Friday and I was glad I was home, but I really missed the people I met in a semester and a half of my first year of college.

The first week home was fine, but then I heard campus wasn't opening for the rest of the semester and I was sad.

The rest of the semester went online and honestly it didn't go well for me and my sister. We had classes at different times so we didn't know when we had to be quiet for one another. It was also difficult in some classes to keep track of assignments without more professor instructions. I missed my on-campus tutor and TRIO advisor, whom I could go to anytime when I needed academic support.

It was an adjustment, but somehow, we got past that and came together to help each other with scheduling and keeping track of my work. I missed the friends I made at CU and the school events and clubs I took part in.

The year in history will be a weird time to remember for all of us, with this pandemic and all the natural disasters that hit in this country the past seven months. But mostly I am grateful to not be affected by the pandemic and to have a family who cares for me and tries to help me get through it. I also like seeing how others continue to care about each other during times of need.

Safe, yes, but missing friends and family

From April to August, we were stuck in homes with nowhere to go. No one could see each other during stressful times and classes were going online. Even with this event happening, there is always hope beyond these dark times.

COVID is a very scary time for the entire world. There are so many unanswered questions about this and my family took precautions for the worst. You see, I live in New Jersey, and we had the second-highest rates of cases until now.

After I left Castleton in March, my family and I stayed home for four months. The state was shut down and we worked and schooled from home. Every night we saw our state numbers on the news and realized how serious this was.

We didn't go anywhere or see anybody for two months. My father did the grocery shopping and my mother went to the pharmacy if needed and we ordered out dinner at least two or three times a week.

Each week, our family would also bring dinner to a group at the hospital as a way of giving back to those in need. We put up thank you signs and balloons to thank all the first responders as part of a town-wide effort.

We had masks made and stocked up on everything we needed to stay safe.

One thing that was hard was not seeing my entire family. We missed some graduations, some family birthdays, and we only saw each other from a distance. Thankfully, no one in my family got COVID, but we all followed the guidelines.

Finally, we had some freedom and took precautions when going back out, and things were kind of going back to normal.

I was so excited when I heard from Castleton that we were allowed to come back on campus. Yes, things are different, but we all are adjusting to what's going on and I'd rather do online classes in my dorm than my home.

Good to be home on campus

Nobody thought coronavirus would hit the United States this fast and affect so many people or that this pandemic would be going on for this long. Since this pandemic first started, everyone has been freaking out and losing their minds in their homes and online.

From March 2020 to today, Oct. 1, 2020, we have been in a pandemic and soon we'll be going into our eighth month. But thankfully, people in most states are trying to improve and adapt for the safety of the citizens in their own states and for the country.

For example, most of the Northeast states were trying their best to flatten the curve.

Also, people are taking every precaution to be safe when outside and to adapt to this new normal, doing things like wearing masks.

For the past two months, I've been back on campus doing remote learning. And since being back, it feels like I'm home again.

Even though this is only my second year on campus, I felt happier because I was able to see some of the people I met last year who returned to live on campus also. I now had my course materials, my campus advisor and tutoring available when needed, but most importantly I was able to access rooms and instruments I could use for my classes.

Even though I'm away from home, I am keeping track of the COVID statistics and what's actually going on in my home state. And the result is a mixed bag.

To be honest, I don't know what's gonna happen after today or into the next few months. I'm just lost in all this, just like all of you reading this.

While still in this pandemic and with the first presidential debate about two days ago, the last three months of 2020 might be a rough ride, but I think and hope we might make it through to the end.

A haunting quarantine

A bunch has been going on since my last blog.

Before Halloween and before this election, I was in quarantine for a week after possibly being exposed to COVID-19.

I went into a quarantine building Monday at 4 p.m. through Friday at 2 p.m.

You might be confused why I was in there for only a week? It was because my friend's roommate wasn't feeling too good and we didn't know if he had COVID or not. So we were required to move into the quarantine building immediately.

Around this time, my parents were freaking out and scared. And to be honest, I was also afraid. There wasn't a lot to do and some say that the building we stayed in was haunted.

Nothing happened to me at least, but my roommate told me he heard voices from the other rooms when no one is there, heard footsteps walking around at night and saw shadows of people at night.

I was surprised he told me all of this, and that he had to get permission from the Wellness Center to leave Friday saying he had to fix his car, but it was really because he just couldn't stay in there for another night.

Another thing that happened Thursday was scarier for both of our sanity when the UVM Medical Center was hacked at an unknown time, giving us more fear about never getting my roommate's test result.

No one knew what was going on. We were kind of losing our minds, but thankfully he was NEGATIVE and I was able to leave that Friday too! The only good thing that came out of this COVID quarantine was the idea for the screenplay assignment, based on a realistic fiction story.

CHAPTER 7

Adrianna Maher

Adrianna got ripped from study-
ing abroad in Meknès, Morocco,
in the spring semester to return to
her northern Vermont home, where
she would hole up with her parents
and two equally worldly sisters. She
often wrote cleverly crafted, reflec-
tive blogs about being thankful,
and about family. But she is also a
master of sarcastic one-liners, like
in her blog about doing pandemic
puzzles.

Pandemic pushes us all back under one roof

COVID-19 became the cause of family reunions worldwide; my family was no exception.

I returned home in mid-March from my study abroad being cut short. In the few weeks following my return, my two older sisters made the decision to come back to Vermont as well.

For two weeks, it was just me and my parents.

Then it was time to pick up one sister flying in from California at the airport. A few weeks after that, we drove halfway between

Burlington and New York City to grab my eldest sister.

By April, our house was full again, much to our mother's delight.

We hadn't truly lived together since 2013, after my eldest sister graduated high school. I won't lie, I slightly dreaded what might happen living with my sisters again. We can get on each other's nerves like no one else. I was afraid of endless bickering and being constantly confined in the same house.

Then the unexpected happened. We actually lived in peace for three months. I still do not know how we managed that. Of course, there were a few comments and tiffs here and there. But nothing too extreme.

COVID-19 gave our family this wonderful time together. It is one of the only positives I can find as a result of these circumstances. We would have never had this time together without the shutdown.

They have since moved back to their lives in separate states. Life moves on even in the midst of a pandemic.

But this summer will always hold a special place in my heart, even though it was the furthest thing from how I saw it going back in January.

Pandemic pavement – and me

I guess I jog now?

Do you remember at the beginning of lockdown, making jokes about going on your daily walk? You have most likely participated in at least one, voluntarily or not.

It was fun at first, getting out of the house and stretching my legs. My sister and I coined it our mom walk. We would bundle up and take on the neighborhood, cups of coffee in hand.

As lockdown kept getting extended, the days merged together. I was passing the same houses and living the same day over and over. My daily walks soon became a couple-times-a-week walk.

I am lucky enough to live in Vermont, where the outdoors isn't hard to come by and yet I wasn't taking advantage of it. It was the one available thing I could do, but I had crossed it off my list.

As the weeks kept progressing, the effect isolation was having on me was increasing.

I finally got to a point of being so fed up physically and mentally that I did the unthinkable: I went on a run.

Now, I have never been a runner. I may have been on the track and field team in high school, but only as a thrower. I never understood how people could enjoy running. Honestly, I still find it hard to believe.

What I believed to be a one-time thing, something just to clear my head, became two runs and then three and then … you get the point.

Never would I have thought *I* would start jogging. Back in April I actually tweeted, "I'm doing my part in this lockdown by not picking up jogging."

Talk about eating your own words. Don't worry; I have since gone back and updated my followers, whom I'm sure really care.

I'm still jogging on the same streets of my former daily walks. For some reason, it just feels different. Maybe it's because the slightly faster pace doesn't allow me time to analyze every little detail.

There really isn't a profound message to this story, just that I got sick of my mundane walks and switched it up for jogging. Which, luckily, turned out to be a bit healthier for me.

Feeling like 2020 was ripped from me

Time keeps passing, no matter how hard I try to slow it down.

I like to call it the coronavirus effect, which may be too vague (I am still workshopping). The monotonous routines, and days with no differentiating features, have caused months to slip through my fingers.

My mind cannot wrap around the fact it's October. Where did the year go?

It doesn't seem plausible that I have been living in my hometown for seven months now. Memories have blended together, no new life events to categorize my year. Looking back, it's hard to visualize the time that has passed.

2020 was ripped from me, months feel like weeks and weeks a few days.

Not to say I haven't enjoyed this time. It has been a period of self-discovery and reconnecting with my family. Yet, I feel as though I'm mourning for what could have been and what I have missed.

I had great things scheduled; most have since evaporated into thin air. But great things have taken their place.

I traded completing my semester abroad for two amazing best friends; a summer working in New York City for a gubernatorial campaign internship; and watching my sister compete in Colorado, for months with my family.

I have missed out on a few things, but it could have been much worse. I recognize this and am unbelievably grateful for what took their places.

The whole world is experiencing its own shifted relationship with time. In my case, time thinks it's late for work and is rushing by.

Taking this "senior" thing a bit far

Let's be real, no one expected a pandemic to happen during their time in college. I sure didn't.

But here I am, back with my parents, doing puzzles on Saturday nights. The kicker is my parents aren't even helping with the puzzle. I chose to start it – it's my fun project for the week.

I think I may be taking this senior thing too literally.

Honestly, I am enjoying it. As long as I don't think too much about what I would be doing if I were on campus for a regular year.

Yes, I miss my friends and have a nagging feeling deep in my stomach that my 20s are slipping away from me. But that's our life now.

The whole romanticizing of youth is overrated anyway. Life is so much more than a handful of years when our brains are still developing.

It's easy to type this but not as easy to wholly believe. We have been fed this narrative from a young age and trying to break from it is proving to be very difficult.

I have high hopes for what lies ahead. This chapter in our lives still has blank pages to be filled, but that's now part of our story. The pandemic will be a defining feature for our generation. Together we mourn what could have been and try to move past the expectations for our youth to look a certain way.

And if anyone has an idea of how I tell my grandmother her puzzle is missing two pieces, please let me know.

A difficult gut decision

Soon after I began at Castleton University, I had already begun outgrowing it.

I was tired of the predictable and monotonous semesters.

Much of it stemmed from what I was used to. I was born and raised in Burlington, Vermont, the largest city in the state. Which, compared to the rest of the U.S., isn't all that big.

However, the move to a town of 5,000 people on a good day was striking. I had also recently spent time abroad, where there was a new experience around every corner.

I feel like I've been counting down the years to graduation since the beginning.

I was ready to get my degree and move on to the next stage of my life.

Then, interestingly enough, COVID-19 in a way gave me what I wanted. No longer did I have to go back to campus. I was free to finish my degree wherever I wanted.

For financial and safety reasons, I chose to stay home with my parents. I believe I made the correct decision, but a part of me can't shake the feeling I'm missing something. That no matter how much I claimed I was ready to move on, I still wanted my time in college.

It is now almost the end of the fall semester and I had to make the decision again. Would I go back to campus or not?

For the second time this year, I made the choice to stay at home. I have a job that pays above minimum wage, a comfortable room, a bathroom I don't share with an entire floor, good food, and loving parents.

This time it doesn't feel like the right decision, though. I want to close out my undergraduate years on campus and with my peers. But with graduation looming and health risks, I have chosen the safer option. I want to follow my gut, but it's difficult to do in the middle of a pandemic.

CHAPTER 8

Lance Robinson

Lance came to the Media Writing class through the College STEPS program for students with varying abilities. He always had a pretty upbeat tone and could be counted on to talk about pro wrestling, Sonic the Hedgehog and student radio in most posts. In his first entry, he spoke briefly about how the pandemic didn't really impact him, then said, "What I really want to talk about is my experience with WWE Thunderdome."  *He was also pretty psyched to return to off-campus apartment living, though, and often offered boiled-down logic about the pandemic.*

Wrestling through a pandemic – WWE style

Even though times are rough right now with COVID-19 and stuff, one thing that I enjoyed is just at least going back to a college dorm. I've been enjoying my time with my new roommates and doing some essential stuff that we need and the list goes on.

For me, whenever I go to the gym at the fitness center at Castleton, I make sure to disinfect everything I use, including the weights and the seats.

On Tuesdays from 11:30 a.m. to 12:30 p.m., I host a radio show on Castleton Internet Radio, but when I enter the studio, I have to wear a facemask for protection.

That stuff happens all around the state of Vermont.

At home, I manage to get in the WWE Thunderdome every Monday and Friday to cheer and boo the wrestlers, including the mystery group known as RETRIBUTION.

One time, on the Sept. 14, 2020 episode of "Raw," I saw myself on TV, especially during the steel cage match. I was so stoked.

I almost cried, but I didn't because I don't like tears, just like Sonic.

Speaking of Sonic, whenever I have time during my stay at my dorm, I hop on YouTube to catch all the episodes of "Sonic X," a TV series that ran from 2003-2006 on FOX's kids lineup FOX Box/4KidsTV. Can't wait to see how this turns out.

When I get bored, I also hop on iHeartRadio to listen to Active Rock 99rock WFRD from the area I live in. I live in a town where "The Simpsons" movie premiere took place, Springfield, Vermont. Also, whenever I have time, I would just play the two "Watchdogs" games on my Xbox One.

Other than that, I've been doing fine at my dorm since my return in August from the five-month hiatus.

Look, the world's not gonna end. It's just a pause to stop the spread of COVID-19.

No other choice

The difference.

Back during my time at college before COVID-19, I used to just go to baseball games, football games and basketball games. Everything was so amazing, being in a classroom, going to watch a play, going to karaoke nights and everything.

I was so amazed. Just going to the Campus Center to talk with friends was fun.

I enjoyed everything at college.

Everyone used to sit next to each other in the Campus Center, but now some chairs are all taped up with signs telling you not to sit on them. Four computers used to operate, but now you can only choose one of two computers because of the distance. The Fireside Café now has to make sure the tables are clean before people can sit to enjoy their meal.

And the facemask, it's everywhere these days.

At the gym, you'd always make sure to sign in before using the gym and sanitize everything you use, but now you have to use your ID to let the gym worker sign you in. Not only that, but you have to use a dish cloth-looking thing to wipe down everything you sanitize after using it.

2020 sucks!

But look, the world's not going to end, it's just a pause in time to stop the spread of the virus, similar to the people of 1918 fighting the Spanish flu.

If we want everything, including schools, to go back to normal, we have to fight it. I know it's hard, but we gotta do it.

We got no other choice.

CHAPTER 9

Jana DeCamilla

Jana technically wasn't in the class, serving as a STEPS mentor to Lance Robinson. But she sat through all the classes and helped him with all his homework, from press releases to radio ads. And when I had the idea to see if she wanted to write a COVID Chronicle for the  *book, she told me she had been secretly bumming she wasn't a part of the project. Now she is, and as a mom of one with another on the way, she offered a very different perspective on COVID-19 life.*

Ode to Lucy

We bought a 2009 Lincoln MKS in mid-March.

It was calling to us from the side of the building as we pulled up to the buy-here-pay-here dealership.

Fresh on the lot that day and not yet looked over by the mechanic, we picked this as our first car together and patiently waited for it to be road-ready.

It has been nine months since then and we have added 40,000

miles and some character to Lucille, as we affectionately named her.

Lucy the Lincoln soon became our inside, outside. We ran from the confines of quarantine and the rapidly spreading virus in our pretty silver beast. Disposable masks, gloves, and hand sanitizers were strewn about the seats and floor, replaced by new packs every week.

We traveled roads that seemed abandoned and saw town after town shut down. We watched as passing cars faded and were replaced by sparse joggers or solitary gardeners kneeling in the sanctuary of their flower beds.

We didn't find new hobbies or redecorate the apartment. We explored behind the engine roar in our bubble of COVID-free air.

Our home offered refuge, where we kept my son, Cire, safe from the germs that threatened to give his 4-year-old asthmatic lungs a fight. But Lucy offered us adventure when the commercial world closed down.

She offered a way to reconnect with old songs we'd forgotten and share stories from pre-pandemic life. We were inseparable before quarantine, but corona gave us the time to just be a family, free from the stresses of work schedules and schoolwork.

We bonded as a blended family of three and began to grow our fourth member.

We've begun to question the space inside our sedan and wondered whether it would continue to accommodate our growing boy and bundle of joy to come.

But we just can't seem to part with the vehicle that brought us solitude, safety and scenery in a time we weren't allowed to go outside.

CHAPTER 10

Jasmin Gomez

Jasmin is another driving force in the decision to compile these blogs into a book, primarily due to her creative post that read like an apology letter to the friends and family she abandoned – out of fear – during the early stages of the pandemic. She struggled with the pandemic, but also wrote about how it brought her closer to her older brother, despite him being 3,000 miles away in  *California. She also helped design the book's cover!*

A teary spring goodbye, but life didn't stop

I remember the morning of Friday, March 13. The night before, we all received the email about a two-week closure due to COVID-19. Looking back now, I can't believe we thought it was just a two-week closure.

I only had one class that Friday. It was quiet; a sense of uncertainty filled the room. There were mixed emotions about what was to come. We talked about COVID, how we felt and the plan when we come back in two weeks.

But that plan never happened, and it won't, as we have moved on to a new semester.

After that class ended, I said my goodbyes to my friends and professors, uncertain if we would actually be back in two weeks.

I went out to my car and sat there in silence. I couldn't even grasp what was going on. I wasn't ready for change and I became scared of what COVID could do. I turned my car on, but I couldn't get myself to leave. At that moment, I realized how important this school was to me and that I loved being here every day.

With teary eyes, I put my car in drive and went home.

Castleton made the right call, despite how hard it was.

I look back at this moment a lot. I feel grateful that Vermont and our Castleton community continue to persevere during these times. But I would be lying if I said I didn't struggle quite a bit during these times. When you lose that sense of control over your life, especially all at once, it damages your spirit.

I've adapted to these changes despite how difficult they've been. But life doesn't stop – even for a pandemic.

I've learned that sometimes we do need a break from our daily lives. It was hard to accept that at first, but it allowed me to take it easy and live freely for the first time in a while.

Bonding with Jesse

COVID brought many families close together, because they were literally crammed into one household. But I found that COVID brought my brother and me closer – despite being on different sides of the country.

My older brother, Jesse, moved out to California a couple of years ago. Between the five-year age gap and three-hour time difference, it has been hard to find common ground in interests and time to talk. Of course, as we've gotten older and been on our own, we have been able to connect more than when we were younger.

If you have an older sibling with a large age gap, you probably know what I mean.

Keeping in touch can be hard for everyone as our daily schedules consume us, but COVID put those schedules to an abrupt halt.

I remember the first time Jesse called me after I told him the news of Castleton closing and losing my job. We talked about what COVID is like in Rutland compared to Lake Tahoe. He said things were pretty safe there because all the tourists were sent home.

Life didn't seem to be too out of the ordinary for him as he continued to do his thing, skateboarding and snowboarding.

I don't think he realized how much that call meant to me.

I was not enjoying online school, and I'm still not.

I was so caught up in losing my job and all the other things I didn't have control over.

I was sad.

I was pissed.

I was just not having it.

But hearing from my brother and being reminded that it is what it is, is what I needed.

My brother has always been the one to pick me up when I was down, whether it was boy problems or just being mad at the world. He also made sure to give me a reality check here and there to let me know my problems aren't as bad as I make them seem.

But that five-minute call felt similar to when he would bring me out to get food or go Walgreens to get Ben & Jerry's when I had a bad day.

I now hear from Jesse about every other week instead of once a month. We catch up and talk about school and jobs. It may be brief and at midnight my time, but it's worth it.

COVID has affected us all in many different ways, but I'm thankful for the way it has bought me closer with my family.

I'm so sorry...

Dear,

Everyone who didn't hear from me from March 2020-September 2020:

I want to start this off saying I hope you're doing well and that you've been safe and healthy. I know I have some explaining to do.

So, hear me out.

I didn't intentionally mean to stop talking to you all at once. COVID fear got the best of me.

It made me into a different person, and as I look back now, I feel super annoyed with myself. So, I understand where you're coming from if you were or still are annoyed with me.

Isolation and the fear that came from COVID took a toll on me. I felt safest when I was alone. I didn't want it to be that way, but it was. I was unaware of how withdrawn I became until now.

I got to a point where I felt fear when seeing some of you. I was worried you could be sick, or I could get you sick. You probably didn't know, but I would watch the numbers of cases and deaths go up every day.

Knowing that people were losing their loved ones made me so scared to lose mine. I was hoping I would watch the numbers start going down one day, and life could get back to normal in a blink of an eye.

I also got too comfortable being alone. I thrived when I didn't have to leave the house. I let the break from school and work manifest into a whole different type of isolation.

I then found it easier to tune out the whole world by deleting my social media apps. I couldn't take the constant reminder of the virus and how many people were dying because of it.

It was gut-wrenching.

Being alone was easier and safer for me.

But I was so unaware of how it would change things in the long run.

I've reconnected with some of you the past couple of weeks. Getting a text back when I don't feel like I deserved one meant a lot. I've learned it is better to come together in times of crisis instead of hiding from the world.

I'm sorry for the birthdays, graduations and other important moments I missed. I was cheering you on from the safety of my home.

I'm ready to create normalcy since it is not something that can be given. So, whether it is FaceTiming, finding a safe way to hang out or getting matching facemasks to re-establish our friendship, I'm here.

With love,

Xoxo

Jasmin

Unfinished mural is fine as it is

Before we were sent home because of COVID, I was taking Mega Pro Studio.

In this class, taught by professor Oliver Schemm, we were hired by the Castleton Science Department to create murals for its part of the building.

We worked on these murals diligently for a couple of weeks.

Then the talk of COVID started.

And then, the email went out about the school closure.

The following day in Mega Studio, we talked about what was going to happen with the murals. Oliver didn't have an answer, which was understandable. There were too many unknowns.

A couple of weeks ago, Oliver mentioned he would like to finish the murals as soon as possible.

I haven't told him this, but I don't want to.

COVID caused life to stop abruptly.

These unfinished murals say a lot. They make a statement. They document the moment where everyone at that campus became affected by COVID.

Part of me doesn't feel right acting as if that moment never happened because it represents a part of history.

It is much more than a mural for the science department. It is a direct representation of how a virus stopped the world, the country and our small campus.

CHAPTER 11

Luke McGee

Luke was clearly the poet of the COVID Chronicles blog. I came to eagerly anticipate his next example of descriptive prose, great pacing and clever use of analogies. And just like his contagious larger-than-life personality, he could be counted on by the class to offer an uplifting look at the pandemic at a time when others couldn't.

Seasons change, but it's different this year

It was a crisp March morning, the air as fresh as the water I cheerfully sipped while striding across campus.

It was finally the start of spring. And after a barren winter, the world was finally beginning to blossom around me. The flowers bloomed, the grass turned green with envy at the flowers' beauty and life finally sprung once again.

But this was not the case in the rest of the world.

There were rumblings.

As if under the viridescent blanket that coated our earth, something ancient was stirring. Whispers and rumors were as contagious as what lurked just beneath. Something was spreading. It had killed thousands and was looking to kill many more.

Back then, I didn't know its name.

Back then it had no weight.

Back then it was spring.

I dutifully arrived right on time to my choral class, reinvigorated by the breath of life all around me.

I laughed with my friends, we got caught up, once again a part of each other's lives.

We sang and then – *"beep, beep, beep!"*

At the end of class, we got a notification and suddenly what had been lurking beneath erupted before us.

There was panic!

How were we getting home?

What would classes look like moving forward?

Is my family safe?

Am I safe?

The life of spring had become a death threat.

Air that was once fresh was now tainted with an invisible killer.

Before we knew it, it was summer.

And as life flourished, the world died.

Every day the death count ratcheted up, hundreds upon thousands of people had suffered brutally unimaginable deaths, and it was only getting worse.

Human connection had been severed, screens stood like jail bars in between each comforting face. So close yet so far.

Now it is fall.

And as nature dies, slowly life begins to return.

How ironic.

The world is out of tune.

Spring means new life, but the life we knew ended.

In summer life flourished, but more and more died.

And as life dies in the fall, our lives find a way.

But alas, I worry – for how long will fall last?
What will we do when the snow falls?

I am a resilient palm tree

Who am I?

While being the title of one of the greatest Broadway musical numbers of all time, it is also a question I have asked myself consistently throughout the course of my entire life; and it seems I am not alone in regard to this inner inquiry.

Little did I know that it would take a worldwide pandemic to finally get my answer.

Let me take you back to a particularly cold day in April of 2020. What had been slumbering underneath the surface had finally burst forth in all its hideous and monstrous ways.

As this creature of darkness ravaged the world, I sat helpless in my bedroom.

As this monster murdered thousands of people, I tried to help in any way I could.

As this beast swept the cowering earth, I realized I was a tree against a hurricane.

But what kind of tree was I?

At first, I felt like a pine tree. Tall and stoic, standing guard but to no avail. I was swept away by the hurricane in an instant.

But this was not true.

Next I thought I was a fruit tree. Allowing brief moments of reprieve and fruit to replenish health, but was left bare and fruitless by the power of the hurricane.

But this also was not true.

After weeks of analysis and months of trying my best to fight against a storm that was so massive in scale there was no way to overpower it, I finally realized what I am: a palm tree.

This hurricane has bent and swayed me in ways too painful and horrifying to survive, yet I am left standing.

And in these times of great uncertainty, we are *all* palm trees.

We have been pushed and pulled and bent nearly to the point of snapping, and yet here we stand.

Here we live.

And here we try to thrive in the midst of a cyclone.

Don't search for a reason for this – there isn't one

"Everything happens for a reason."

To this day, whenever I hear that quote, I am overtaken by an overwhelming sense of dread.

I would like to believe we live in a perfectly planned-out world, where every action has a preconceived consequence manifest-destiny style. It makes the weight of decision making and free will much less daunting. But I must raise the argument: did more than a million people die worldwide from coronavirus for, quote, *"a reason?"*

The answer, I believe, is no.

There is no reason for the horrors and despair of this world. We desperately grasp for explanations where there are none, like we're caught in a riptide; desperately grasping at sand only to find that it drifts away with us. But what a worldwide pandemic has taught me is that how we arrived at a moment is less important than how we react to it.

In October of 2020, there are so many moments challenging us, dragging us farther and farther from the shoreline, plunging us into uncertain waters. We have not lost people to this riptide for a *reason*, riptides are not personal; thus, we need to stop exhausting ourselves fighting the tide that brought us here.

It's time to embrace the lessons of survivors caught in a force they cannot beat head on. In a riptide, you fight the pull by swimming along the shoreline instead of back the way you came.

But the riptide is not the *reason* people choose to fight, they choose to fight because they believe that maybe, just maybe, that next spot along the shoreline can be better than the last.

This perseverance, this adaptation, this hope; this is not manifest destiny.

Saying that fighting the riptide "was meant to be" is an injustice to the humans who fought for a new way to survive.

Over 1 million people did not suffer lonely and breathless deaths for *a reason*.

Over 7 million people did not come close to this same fate for *a reason*.

The world was not thrust into the throes of death for *a reason*.

But this attempt to thrive in a time when just surviving seems impossible? This attempt to find a better place along the shore?

We are the "reason" for that.

Surrounded by whale lines – and surviving

Every day of our lives we are hunting whales.

We pursue ideals and beliefs far too large for us to fathom in an attempt to make meaning out of this thing we call life. And thus, danger comes with the territory.

We ride in minuscule boats that stray ever farther from the relative safety of our ship.

We approach a leviathan with malicious intent.

We try to survive when that intent is realized by a giant.

As we desperately row in pursuit of the behemoth, our hands brush against the whale line, slack and meaningless, for all focus is centered upon rowing to the rhythm of those around us. Until without warning, that first harpoon strung with the whale line is thrust into the whale – and all hell breaks loose.

The whale line leaps into action, going at neck-breaking speeds inches from our limbs, attaching us to the leviathan, which now drags us along at its will.

And as we try to throw lance after lance into this colossus, our boat viciously rocked by the behemoth's mad dash toward freedom, we must avoid being cut in half by a line that presented no danger mere seconds ago.

"All men live enveloped in whale lines. All are born with halters round their necks; but it is only when caught in the swift, sudden turn of death, that mortals realize the silent, subtle, ever-present perils of life" (Melville, 1851).

A harpoon was released in March of 2020, and ever since that fateful month, we have been surrounded by whale lines whisking past us, threatening to make us a memory.

This worldwide pandemic has made us realize "the silent, subtle, ever-present perils of life," and as I read Herman Melville's "Moby Dick," I cannot help but draw myriad connections to our current situation.

Fascinating how a book written in 1851 does a better job of describing the inherent vulnerability and danger we all feel right now than any one of us living in it ever could; for these are universal truths.

We have lost many to the leviathan to which we are currently tied to. People we love, people we loved. And yet those of us left in the boat continue to throw lance after lance in an attempt that seems futile to anyone who may bear witness to it.

Why?

Because we know what waits for us on the shore. Because we know the minute we stop fighting is the minute the whale whips around and snaps our boat in twain with its maw. Because we know that this is a battle worth fighting.

For though we are surrounded by whale lines, we live on.

We await a needed change

It was a crisp March morning, the air as fresh as the water I cheerfully sipped while striding across campus.

It is a rainy November night, the rainfall as heavy as the weight we all carry while we try to survive.

It has been exactly 245 days since COVID-19 was declared a pandemic.

It has been exactly nine months since the rain started to fall.

I still remember that crisp March morning, though it feels years away.

That was March 11 and today is November 11. Happy anniversary to a world in ruin.

For the past four months, I have documented my journey through a worldwide pandemic with COVID Chronicles. I have coped through palm trees and riptides and whales, carefully crafting analogy after analogy as a means of discovering myself and the world around me.

But this final analogy encapsulates it all: it is the rain.

It rains often. It rains hard. It rains gently. It rains constantly. It grows palm trees, causes riptides, falls upon whales and all in between.

Rain is a constant, a comfort to some or a curse to others but a constant all the same.

It brings with it growth and fruition, but also death and destruction.

The rain is but an agent.

Of chaos or health, it can depend upon the day. But we all saw the rain in the months before March. Those rumblings I discussed, the invisible killer.

Just because it was invisible doesn't mean it wasn't there. We were uncertain of the rain's intentions, and it brought with it a hurricane. Many drowned, many drifted, all felt the ramifications.

Now we float amongst the displaced sea and deadly debris.

And we wait.

We await the agent to whisk away the rain.

We await the thing to dry our clothes and dry our tears.

We await the sign to tell us that things may just get better.

We await what always ends the rain ... the sun. And tonight, on this rainy, dreary November night nine months from that fateful morning: I saw the sun.

I looked into the eyes of a close friend and found it.

Where and when I least expected it – I found the sun. It dried my eyes and lifted my head. It taught me the world will never return to the way that it once was.

For the hurricane has torn it to shreds.

It taught me that we've lost too many. If they cannot return, neither can the world. But it taught me that returning is different from adapting. Which is what the world must do for us all to move ahead.

The rain began on a morning in March. We became resilient palm trees torn by a hurricane. The hurricane created riptides, which dragged us all in. In these riptides we found giants, leviathans too large to defeat.

And as we arrive 245 days later at a different place along the shore, we remember how it all began. For it all began with the rain...

Thus it must end with the sun.

CHAPTER **12**

Richard Berry

Rich hates everything about this pandemic and was pretty vocal about it – and about the fact he didn't love this tedious assignment that made him recall pandemic hate. He even gave us a little scare in one entry, one that seemed a little darker than the others, but when I approached him about it, he assured me he has a dark sense of humor and was being largely sarcastic. He also had a forceful final message about the vaccine and moving on.

When it's over, never say COVID-19 again!

Since COVID is all anyone on the news or in life has been talking about for the past six months, it must be the height of luxury to be allowed to think about anything else for just one minute of the day before the next inevitable corporate ad hits me with a fake cheerful message stating "how much we care."

I was only just starting to feel like I had a life; I moved out of my

58

parents' place into a dorm, made multiple travel plans over the summer and had talks of going on tour with my band, just to be forced back home at the last minute to sit and rot indefinitely.

Over the months, I've made various feeble attempts at getting into spirituality and meditation, but I'm not the kind of person who can be happy just sitting and doing nothing.

I'm watching the rest of the world starting to live normal life again while America is being run by a fanatical religious death cult, and I don't even have the option to leave! This has made me twice as angry and temperamental as I've ever been in my life.

Sure, I have a few escapes, but I can only hike, kayak, play video games and watch TV for so many hours before it starts to get old. My once-favorite hobbies have become empty, mindless chores to do for the sake of doing something.

I'm only taking online classes out of boredom. I really can't stand them and there's not going to be any jobs when I graduate anyway.

Sorry I can't be more positive. Maybe there's a minuscule chance something good will come out of it, but I'm tired of talking about it and I'm tired of hearing about it. When it's over, I don't ever want to hear any mention of it again; no mementos, no throwbacks, it doesn't even deserve a passing thought.

A job and a scare

When I got sent home in the spring, I spent the following two months working from midnight to 8 a.m. every night with only a day or two off a week. I went to bed around 9 a.m. and woke up around 3-4 p.m., giving me two or three hours of daylight each day.

My job was to sit alone in a motel office for eight hours watching computer screens with multiple camera views. Mostly I was watching YouTube videos or doing homework. I'm not what you would describe as a workaholic, but there was not much else to do so I figured I would make some extra cash for when it's over.

On my days off, I would hike or hang with a select few friends.

The only jobs available at the time were in highly risky places like hospitals or hotels full of the homeless or COVID-positive patients. I've had my fair share of strange conversations with homeless people while working, like one woman who cried when I told her I don't have cigarettes for her to borrow.

But on this job, I rarely interacted with other people except when taking over a shift.

This motel is reserved for homeless people; some have COVID, some don't. The only thing that scared me out of my cycle of perpetual night was when I talked to somebody staying there.

He came looking for a phone charger and I was close to him without a mask on. I had a mask, I just didn't grab it for some reason. I didn't think anything of this interaction.

A few days later, I saw a note stating this same man was sent to the hospital with COVID symptoms.

I completely freaked out for days. Every time I coughed or sneezed, I thought it was a sign that death was just over the horizon.

Until I finally got a negative test.

I haven't worked that shift since then. But imagine being a nurse in a place like New York City seeing hundreds of patients every day.

I used to check the infection numbers each day expecting it would be over in a few weeks, but I've long since given up.

I don't care what the numbers are anymore. I'm only going to be disappointed if I find out.

Feeling a little selfish

It's strange how I live in the safest state in the country right now, but I keep ending up in the south, the current epicenter.

Just from looking at the numbers, you would imagine there are wagon trains being pulled through the street piled with corpses with a man yelling "bring out yer dead," but there doesn't appear to be any great catastrophe happening.

I'm sure in the hospitals it would be a different story, but just walking around here in South Carolina and earlier in the summer in Tennessee, about half of everyone outside I see is wearing a mask. All businesses require one if you want to go inside and some places have quite a few people but are not completely packed.

Myrtle Beach was once one of the worst places to be, but it's the end of the season, which means it's slightly safer, and it's my last chance to enjoy the beach before it gets too cold.

Some might be horrified to hear we're hanging out in the South with family from Georgia, but don't worry: When I get back home I'll pay the price with a test that feels like someone shoved a shotgun up my nose and pulled the trigger.

Nothing can be enjoyed without an underlying sense of guilt and impending doom. The only defense is an apathetic approach to life. I don't really care what happens in the world anymore, only what happens in my small little bubble.

When the escape is no longer better than reality

This assignment is getting really old and I'm quickly running out of things to talk about. It has gone from beating a dead horse to beating the skeleton of a horse.

Just one would have done the trick just fine.

It'll be interesting to see what happens this winter when it's too cold to go outside and too dangerous to go inside.

I already hate winter enough as it is.

My four main activities during the winter are getting drunk at bars, getting drunk at house parties, getting drunk at home, with skiing coming in fourth. Getting drunk at home is fun for the first 10,000 times, but it gets old after a while.

Some people become alcoholics during quarantine, but I've just drank so much that it took all the fun out of it for me.

If anything, I drink less than I used to, not because of a desire to improve myself but because it's the most boring drug ever made. What's the point in escaping from reality when the escape is not any better?

I wish I could have wasted a whole year of my life in a more interesting and dramatic way than this.

If I had to choose a disaster to live though, I wish we could have an invading foreign army destroying America instead of a disease.

The same number of people would die but at least you can shoot whatever's causing you problems, and those unhinged redneck militias would finally make themselves useful.

Be smart, get the vaccination

We live in a constant state of limbo.

You'd be delusional to think you can just make plans to go somewhere or do something and expect it to actually happen. The only two constants in life are weed and dead-end Tinder conversations.

When I walk down the street, I see the surreal scene of both inflatable snowmen and skeletons, a good symbol that nobody knows what time it is or even cares.

You might as well put up decorations for every holiday since the only way to celebrate is by sitting inside and eating, just like I do every other day of the year.

I'm very happy to hear about the new vaccine being tested and possibly being distributed in December, but for it to work, that would require that at least half of Americans be smart enough to accept it, which seems very unlikely to me.

Even the general in charge of distributing the vaccine said he is afraid not enough people will choose to take it. I personally would crawl over broken glass and burning coals to get a hold of one of those little vials, just so I can move on with my life.

We worked for thousands of years to create things like vaccines and understand how germs and viruses work. We have instant access to all of human knowledge in history.

But we are not any smarter than we were in the 1300s.

My advice to whoever is reading this in the future is that vaccines are a rare privilege that our ancestors didn't have and I know what it's like to go without.

If you can get one, don't be an ungrateful little bitch and just take it.

CHAPTER 13

Anna DiFiore

Anna lives just down the road from me and I've known her since she was little. She's a bit shy, but really found a unique writing voice with these blogs and offered an interesting mix of topics, including missing her enlisted boyfriend and a neat family effort to beat the COVID blues.

Welcomed return to the cousin green room

It was a dreary morning in March when New York Governor Andrew Cuomo appeared on my television. My mom and I were sitting on the couch having a late breakfast while watching his daily briefing.

That was when he announced there would be no more gatherings of any size.

It came as a shock.

Ever since we moved closer to family 14 years ago, we had spent every Sunday night at my Mimi's house for dinner.

As soon as you walk into her little yellow house, you can smell everything she has made.

Stepping into her kitchen, you can see Mimi walking around a table crammed with food while she finishes cooking.

Then there's the living room where grandparents, aunts and uncles are squeezed onto the couch, in every chair and spilling onto the floor.

There's also what we call the green room.

It used to be painted green but since then it has been blue and yellow.

The name stuck.

In the green room is where all the cousins and friends who tag along eat.

Like the living room, there are people sitting wherever they can, the youngest ones often getting stuck on the floor.

The green room is where I have made some of the best memories with my cousins.

The memories from Sunday dinners that lie ahead were taken away with the governor's announcement.

No more laughing at "90 Day Fiancé," which the boys reluctantly watched while we all ate.

No more Wiffle ball games in the backyard between dinner and dessert.

No more teasing each other over anything and everything.

And no more memories in the green room.

Months passed.

We all spent every Sunday night at our own houses, separated by the pandemic.

Then it was finally phase four.

Governor Cuomo announced there could be gatherings of 25 people.

That is all we needed.

That Sunday we all reunited again.

Mimi resumed her position in the kitchen, the parents in the living room and the cousins in the green room.

Everyone was impatient to have Sunday dinners back and finally there was a little sense of normalcy.

TikTok trend turned new family tradition

It was just another day in quarantine.

Spent my day in pajamas, lying in bed, scrolling through TikTok until my brain melted.

There was a trend I had seen going around on the app where families would have some fun by doing themed dinners.

Later that day, my sister suggested our family do the same.

Our parents thought it would be a fun way to break up the monotony and make a good memory out of a bad situation.

The next day, we were having our first themed dinner.

We decided on a fancy, black-tie theme.

When 5:30 p.m. rolled around, my dad got home from work and it was time to get ready.

I picked an old prom dress from high school to wear.

Its maroon lace and scattered sparkles were a perfect fit for the night.

I threw on a pair of heels, did a little makeup and headed to the kitchen.

There my mom was, setting the table in her blouse, maxi skirt and wedges.

Then came my sister, in a long black dress.

Followed by my brother who was complaining about having to wear a tie and put on something besides sweats.

My dad came downstairs in his tan suit and left to go pick up our dinner, undoubtedly getting looks walking into the restaurant so dressed up.

On the menu tonight, contrary to our fancy theme, was O'Tooles.

Takeout from a sports pub.

By the time he got home, the candles were lit, fancy restaurant music was playing softly in the background and our hungry stomachs were impatiently waiting for our chicken fingers.

While we ate, we talked, laughed and reminisced about life before coronavirus.

After that dinner, we decided to continue the fun and do a different theme every Saturday.

The themes that followed included Hawaiian night, sports night, pajama night and U.S.A. night.

It only lasted a month, but my mom decided we will make it an annual event and include the whole family.

Now we will always have a little night in memory of quarantine.

We never thought ...

I don't think anybody thought coronavirus would hit the United States the way that it has.

I remember right before the outbreak, I was at the airport with my boyfriend, Casey, and his mom, dropping him off for Navy boot camp.

At that time, the only talk of the disease was about how it was happening on the other side of the world.

We joked to not breathe in other people's air.

That's all it was though.

A joke.

There was no way anything serious could come of some disease that was all the way in China.

Looking back on that moment, if you had told me then that everything that has happened would happen, I wouldn't have believed it.

We never thought schools would shut down.

Never thought sports would be canceled.

Never thought we would miss Casey's boot camp and A School graduation.

Never thought the whole country would be shut down.

Never thought of anything.

Just joked.

I know I am not alone when I think about how incredible it will be to gather in large crowds again.

To hug and kiss loved ones without worry again.

To watch live sports again.

And to live without a mask.

I can't wait to go back to how life was before.

Carefree.

Happy.

And back to normal.

Dorm life still on hold

I went to a college 10 minutes from my house for two years. I lived at home and drove to school every day.

After I graduated from SUNY Adirondack with an associate's degree in May, I was excited and eager to begin getting ready for school at Castleton.

It was going to be my first time living on a college campus.

I spent my summer ordering everything I wanted, making checklists and working so I could afford everything I needed for school in the fall.

I got new bedding, shower essentials and décor – everything a girl needs to make her dorm feel like home.

As the days of quarantine dragged on and there was no sign of the virus letting up, I slowly lost hope about moving to campus.

When the school announced there would be no in-person classes, I was upset but not distraught.

I knew that was coming.

But the thought of missing out on my first semester away from home was a bit discouraging.

So there my untouched dorm stuff sits, on standby in my dining room in cardboard boxes, waiting hopefully for the spring semester.

I thought I would be in my dorm room right now, experiencing a college campus for the first time.

But here I am, in my room, which I unexpectedly rearranged to accommodate a new desk and chair for my oh-so-exciting online learning.

Here's to a very different 2021

The coronavirus for me has been, for a lack of better words, a nuisance. It has gone on forever. There is no end in sight. Loved ones are scared. And it has been in the news every day since the start, eight months ago.

Exhausting.

Below is a brief recap of almost everything that has happened since March, after COVID-19 began.

Australia bushfires; impeachment trial of President Trump began; stock market crash; 2020 Summer Olympics postponed until 2021; gas cost less than $2 per gallon; Black Lives Matter protests and rioting every day and night for weeks; Ebola outbreak; "Murder Hornets" arrived in America; Beirut, Lebanon explosion; wildfires raged along the West Coast; Ruth Bader Ginsburg passed away; President Trump tested positive for COVID-19; and a second COVID wave is seemingly on the way, if not already here.

The number of things that have happened this year is enough for a decade. And we still have to make it through the last two months of the year.

Like everyone else, I spent the first few months of the pandemic locked up in my house.

Just trying to make the most of a bad situation.

My daily excitement consisted of going to the post office to mail a letter to my boyfriend, who was in Navy boot camp at the time.

Wearing a mask, of course. And sweats, the uniform of everyone in quarantine.

Once summertime hit and the pandemic seemed to be slowing down, I went out more. Not just for necessary trips to the grocery store anymore. I got to go to Target to look around.

It was exciting. And simultaneously nerve wracking. I got to work again, hang with friends again (from a distance) and see other family members besides the ones in my house.

We are now in November and the coronavirus is still very much a threat. It is difficult to decipher whether we are less worried about the disease or if we are learning to live with this new normal.

Either way, I am hoping that 2021 brings us back to life before mask mandates, before limits on gathering sizes and before the world shut down. Back to life before COVID-19.

CHAPTER 14

Marty Kelly III

Marty brought a different perspective to the class, one shared by many in the country who feel that basic rights were being stripped from citizens in the name of the pandemic. He is also a race car driver, and offered an uplifting glimpse of the power of people in the stands.

The bright, silver, aluminum elephant in the room

Where have all the fans gone?

Albany-Saratoga Speedway is one of the premier dirt oval racing facilities in the state of New York. It's affordable and its delicious concessions, clean restrooms, incredible announcing and stout field of modified division drivers make it standing room only on Friday nights.

Its capacity is 4,000 in the general admission stands with well over 1,000 more in the pit area, where people walk among behemoth tractor-trailer haulers, professional drivers and rusty half-ton pickups with open trailers for hobby racers.

This year, the season started in June, two months later than usual. And that first qualifying race was bizarre.

I went out toward the tail, started maybe sixth, seventh or eighth. The car was good, and I was confident, but something was weird.

It should not have been a surprise, but it felt that way anyway. We charged out of the fourth turn for the green flag, and the bleachers were practically blinding.

They are not in our field of view, but if you look to the right you can see them, and they were totally empty.

Not a soul.

A huge, bright, silver aluminum elephant in the room.

There aren't any fans here; they're not allowed.

Every Friday, we raced in front of nobody. They watched at home on pay-per-view. That was all the people could do.

Fast-forward to Labor Day Weekend. West Haven, Vermont's Devil's Bowl Speedway has allowed fans most of the season. The grandstands are only allowed 750 people, but hundreds more watch from their vehicles in the infield, tailgate style.

I've always appreciated the fans, but this was even more special. On the final parade lap before I and 33 others embarked on a straining journey of 200 laps, 100 miles, the fans saluted us as we waved to them. Seven-hundred and fifty people held up cell phones and their flashlights illuminated the scene.

They waved them back and forth and all over – and it was a special thing.

I can't describe how it made me feel. I was so grateful they were there, and they mirrored that gratitude.

I can't wait for fans to be back in the stands in New York, where we can go see them and talk to them and share the magic of motorsports with people in person.

It was more than a game for them

It wasn't even a nice night.

It was cold and damp, rain came down heavily at times; the kind of night when people sit inside and read or watch a movie.

County Street is pretty long. It runs from Benmont Avenue, up to

Branch Street. Blocks 100-1000. I guess the whole thing is probably half a mile or a little longer. It's long compared to the quaint side streets that run off it, like Maple, Division, Charles, Grove, and all the rest.

It borders Mount Anthony Union High School on the south side, where the green grass is; at the 500-block, it runs along the baseball and softball fields, and at the 700-block, the football field.

A chain link fence separates the high school's grounds from the eight-foot gravel patch on the side of County.

I drove toward Bradford Street, in that 1000-block, from a delivery somewhere else, listening to the Yankees game, hoping they would lose.

I saw cars and trucks lined up all down County Street, in the eight-foot patch of gravel.

People, watching a Vermont D-2 high school football game in the rain, were standing in truck beds and sitting next to cars in lawn chairs.

The state approved high school sports last week, without fans. The fans did not approve high school sports without fans, however, and they found their loophole. Mount Anthony gave them a show, too. Senior quarterback Caleb Hay threw for 446 yards, including a 14-yard score to senior receiver Gavin Johnson. They beat Otter Valley 48-19.

The scoreboard faces exactly away from where those people watched the game. The field is at least 30 yards from the fence line, I'll bet.

I don't know what this means aside from that people like football, and parents want to see their kids' senior seasons.

I think it means more than that.

A lot more.

Hoping it doesn't change the holidays – too much

I don't even know what to write about at this point. I guess I'll spitball a little bit and touch on a few different things.

I was very glad to receive an email on the university president's behalf this morning. Things are moving in the right direction it appears, and we will be able to have some in-person learning in the spring.

You know, something just hit me pretty hard, actually. What's going to happen with Christmas and Thanksgiving?

For the none of you who know me, you know that my favorite time of year is unquestionably November 20-ish through New Year's Day. The holiday season has long been my favorite. Thank goodness this fall semester ends at Thanksgiving, because I tend to not do much work for school during that time.

I like seeing my family, without masks.

I enjoy Black Friday and trips to the mall for shopping. I enjoy Christmas Eve mass at St. John's, right across the street from campus. Most of my family, or half, still lives in Castleton.

I've always loved the winter and so much of that is interaction with people. I can't wait for this COVID deal to be done. I'm not looking forward to a different-looking winter.

I hope that this country isn't too tired to celebrate, decorate and do all the things we love this Christmas.

The restrictions were infringing on rights

It seems like you're not allowed to have the opinion that the COVID-19 restrictions are, at the very least, a restriction on some of the most basic rights of Americans in this day and age.

So, I won't tell you that's what I think.

But I will tell you many people have suffered fates worse than death because of the government regulations in place. How many businesses closed? Those are people's means of earning a living.

You used to be free to pursue happiness.

That pursuit is a process that includes going to work or operating a business so you can keep your head above water. Before they told us we could no longer get haircuts, I sat in a barbershop with two men in April, each about 60 years old.

They both owned restaurants forced to close, and couldn't afford to reopen. Those guys worked hard, had retirement plans wrapped up in stocks and bonds that disappeared almost overnight when the economy collapsed.

They're probably bagging groceries right now, if they could find a job at all, and probably will until they die. You gave people the option to vote by mail, you can get anything delivered to your house, anyone who is susceptible to this virus has a right to close themselves off entirely.

But the rest of us could have gone wherever, whenever.

Wearing masks for those of us out would be a reasonable compromise, I think. But we shut everything down, made everyone stay in their state, even in their county. California made them stay in their homes and threatened to cut off basic utilities like water and electricity to anyone violating gathering rules.

Mental health struggles increased, along with substance abuse and depression. Those things come from lost jobs and being trapped inside your house all the time. There is no vaccine for suicide, but at least we put the whole country "on pause" like a video game at dinner for a disease that 97 to 99.75 percent of people recover from (WebMD).

By the way, would it have killed to let the NFL have a pre-season? The Giants have an entirely new staff, and they've only won five games so far.

This piece serves not to downplay the severity of COVID-19. I know and miss a few folks who passed away due to its aggressive nature and fast spread. I am simply examining in hindsight what may have been done differently to improve the overall situation for the rest of the country moving forward, and the seldom-discussed adverse effects of lockdowns and restrictions.

CHAPTER 15

Lukas Carlson

Lukas is another Castleton football player who, like Jacob, struggled at times through the pandemic with COVID-19 fear. He longed to be able to go home, but restrictions prohibited it. He struggled with missed birthdays, missed football games, missed family. He also settled into COVID-19 life, but only briefly, before returning to uncertainty and more fear.

Life is on hold

This has been possibly the most historic year of our lives thus far. Our whole world has been altered from the ways of life we have grown so accustomed to for so long.

And it's not easy to deal with.

I keep a saying in the back of my mind: "Historic times create historic people."

Pretty sure I just made it up, but it's true.

Summer has always been the best season, for a multitude of

reasons. In Saratoga, New York, it means the opening of the racing season; six weeks of horse betting at the nation's oldest operational track.

It means profitable seasonal work was plentiful and very easy to find.

It means long nights drinking on Caroline Street, which is packed door to door with bars suited for any drinker.

It means big parties with all my friends and family, and road trips to see friends in other states.

But all of that is on hold for now.

A scary attack

My birthday was the Fourth of July, and I stressed for weeks if I should even have this party, beyond scared of the repercussions if even just one person somehow needed a test and it came back positive.

I was very skeptical to even see my mom after I would be done working in Vermont and returning home to New York. I couldn't bear how I would feel if I was responsible for infecting my mom and forcing her to take two weeks off from her job (she is only working one, after expecting to be working three this summer).

The pandemic has taken a huge toll on the population's mental health, whether people want to realize and accept that or not.

I had a terrible anxiety attack that lasted a few days. I had convinced myself I was exhibiting symptoms and my mind just took over my body.

I was having horrible chest and heart pains, like a fist was wrapped around my heart and it was getting squeezed like a stress ball.

My heart rate was pounding at full speed constantly, and nothing I did would help it.

Frantically, I made it back home and got checked out by two doctors. Both gave me a clean bill of health.

My heart rate at the first doctor was somewhere around 140/96 or something like that, which is hypertension.

Thankfully, I am OK now, but a little more cautious than before to take note of my own mental health.

Mom's birthday – without mom

I can't go home.

I live only an hour away from all the things I love the most.

My mom, my house, my bed. Multiple options for takeout food.

I used to be able to make weekend trips home and be able to walk my dog and see my longtime friends.

But I can't anymore, not for a while it seems.

Saratoga County is a "yellow" county, according to the state of Vermont's travel map restrictions.

That means if I go home, and come back to Castleton, I am facing a two-week-long quarantine.

Two weeks of being stuck in my room. Two weeks of not making money. Two weeks of not being able to coach or even go outside.

I think it has been a good month since I have been home. A month since I have seen the sunset on Saratoga Lake.

A month since I have been able to hear stories from my mom, about the great times she and her siblings had at our camp while my Nana was still alive.

The COVID fall season seems to be consuming me, and others, in every aspect.

It is overwhelming, to say the least.

It's my mom's birthday today. I planned earlier in the summer to drive down and surprise her, maybe cut the grass for her or cook her dinner.

But that's on hold, just like every other comfort or shred of normalcy that once was.

When will we return to normal? What is "normal?" Will life ever be the same as it was before the pandemic?

I have caught myself slipping into the same, mundane routine almost every day.

Wake up late, before class.

Get through class, spend $10 on two breakfast sandwiches from Birdseye Diner.

Eat overpriced breakfast. Take depression nap until work.

Wake up, put on the branded polo shirt, then drive 45 minutes to work.

Stay there an hour after closing because some drunken, privileged tourists feel special being in a restaurant after closing.

Slam one mixed drink, buy another for the road.

Get home around midnight, I am *lucky* to get home before 11 p.m.

Finish second mixed drink.

Brush teeth.

Turn on Netflix. Same show I've watched hundreds of times over.

Sleep. Wake up. Do it all over again.

When will it stop? Do I have enough power in myself to make it stop?

How much longer? When can I regain power of my schedule?

Time will have to tell, I guess.

A break from anguish and a glimmer of thankfulness

Relatively settling in?

I have shockingly found myself becoming more and more adjusted to the schedule and customs of life during a pandemic.

After a good week and a half of struggling, a slow but steady rhythm has developed.

It's starting to provide a sense of comfort, knowing when I have class and what I have to do for it.

Knowing exactly where I need to be or what I need to be doing every day (most of the time).

Knowing what off days I can look forward to, instead of waiting for the day to come.

I have found myself not really thinking back on what our "normal" was. I try not to dwell on the past.

Instead, I try thinking to the future, of when our "normal" will return.

Watching the presidential debate did not help with that.

It's clear there is no definite time when we will return to normal, and the two prospective "leaders" who have the most power are only concerned with one another.

But for now, I think I'm OK.

I think I got some shit figured out.

I am still alive, healthy and making money.

I am surrounded by good friends and mentors.

I get to do and be around what I love the most – football – almost every day, even if it is with a mask on that makes my upper lip incredibly sweaty during practice.

Even if there are no pads, no games, no fans, no rivalries.

It is simply football. Just like how life right now is simply life.

It is fall now, there is no denying that.

Fall is normally my favorite season, because of football.

Now it is my favorite because I know winter is coming.

I think I'll reach a moment of clarity, nirvana, epiphany, whatever you want to call it, when I get on my first chairlift ride at Killington.

That is something I do every year, no matter what is going on around me.

It is perhaps one of the few shreds of "normal" I – and many of us – have left. And that still may be in jeopardy.

Regardless, I am here, we are here, healthy and surviving.

I am thankful I am in this world right now, no matter how it seems to be falling around all of us at once.

Life is hard and I want to go home

It is now November. The sun sets earlier, the temperatures are colder.

And COVID is still a threat.

So much of a threat, that now Vermont has removed the leisure travel map, meaning anyone who leaves Vermont and returns has a mandatory 14-day quarantine or a seven-day quarantine and a negative test.

Meaning, if I want to see my family for the first time since late July, I have to sit in my apartment alone for at least a week.

At least a week of no socializing.

At least a week of not being able to make money.

It is November. Hundreds of thousands have died. And I still have to wade through bodies having a party in my kitchen when I get home from work.

I still shudder when the restaurant I work at has a parking lot full of cars, with license plates from red states. Texas. Virginia. New Mexico. Florida. Georgia.

My heart rate increases every time I sneeze, blow my nose or cough, even though I know it's a smoker's cough.

I want to go home.

I want to be home.

I want to be away from all this, but if I go home, I could make everything much worse. What if I am asymptomatic? What if I spread it to my mother, and then she can't work?

I cringe when my roommates don't wash their hands, or cover their mouths when they cough. I know they don't always wear masks. I know they travel.

Do they even care about this shit? I've had two scares already this fall semester. One was a real scare that turned into a negative test. The other was purely driven by anxiety. And I feel I could fall back into that at any second.

New medicine didn't help, so I stopped taking it.

Now the effects of suddenly stopping the medicine are piling up and mixing with everything involved with COVID.

Life is hard.

Life has been hard.

How much longer will our lives be like this? I've caught myself thinking of what to do if I ever find myself tubed up in a hospital bed.

Donate or sell all my belongings if it looks like that's the way I will die. I plan to leave this world with nothing, just like how I came in.

CHAPTER 16

Ryan Phillips

Ryan was one of the few students in class to live on campus for the all-online Fall 2020 semester. And while he writes about enjoying a little dorm-life normalcy, he also frequently wrote about being very angry – until he found love.

I had such big plans

I can't say I know of a single person who has enjoyed the re-percussions of COVID-19. Life is not at all what it used to be. I'm thankful that Castleton is allowing us to be on campus, despite the inconvenience of online learning.

But being a CA this year is certainly giving me another reason to be here, at least, justifying it in my father's mind.

He may not have wanted me to come back, but god, I had to!

Being on campus with only about 400 students is an eerie feeling. For one, there's so much parking. I love it!

On the other hand, everywhere you look, you see nobody. Even Huden Dining Hall is empty, but that's probably for the best.

I'm a CA in the houses, which is pretty much in the back corner of campus. The quiet is great, but incredibly heightened with the current attendance. Nearly all of my friends came back, which is so great for me mentally. I have one as a roommate and it has been quite an adventure, but a worthwhile one.

Classes are going pretty well, at least for me. While there's not a lot to really do as of now, my focus for work hasn't been altered for the worse quite yet. Sure, it could greatly improve, but why rock that boat right now?

I had such big plans for this year, and they were almost instantly ruined. Whether it was my first concert for my favorite band or an exciting vacation, it didn't matter. So whatever the opposite of a shout-out is, I give that to you, COVID-19.

Thanks for ruining everyone's year.

I didn't want to be back

On March 12, we received that dreaded email.

On the night of March 12, I packed my car full of everything important to me. For some reason, I really just wanted to get up and leave the next day, but I didn't want to go home.

I begrudgingly sat through my terrible English class, and it was time.

We had just gotten back from break. Essentially my entire ski team was in Lake Placid at Nationals. What was going to happen to them? Would they cancel the remaining races? What about their massive planned party? Would they have to quarantine somewhere?

But that wasn't my problem.

I left for home, and two hours later, I made it there. As I backed into my driveway, both my parents came out.

There was silence until eye contact was made.

"This is fucking bullshit," I angrily stated.

I received more silence and a head nod.

I have a really good home life.

I don't have an issue with my parents, or my family. I'm truly lucky to have a stable and sound relationship with them. The issue was that I had just been home.

And I didn't want to be back.

I'm on the ski team here at Castleton, and my season had just ended. While my entire team was away winning everything, the other three of us were done and free to do whatever. I wanted to be a belligerent freshman. I hadn't done anything in months, especially after the mess of Halloween, but that's a tale for another time.

I felt deprived. I felt robbed. I felt like the world was out to get me. But, I was only a freshman.

I didn't even feel empathy for high school or college seniors. Or the young elementary children who were confused by the world.

I'd like to think I'm not a cocky or pompous person. I have zero things to be cocky about. I hate myself most of the time, but I felt zero for seniors.

I only cared about me, and rage filled me for months.

That rage continued until August. So much rage.

It's too electric not to

Rage.

A feeling I know all too well.

I like to think of myself as a relatively normal mood kinda dude. I laugh at too many unfunny things, and I have a fair amount of interests.

One of those interests is music.

Loud music.

Heavy music.

Loud and heavy music.

Growing up, I was subjected to a lot of Lithium, which is '90s hard rock and grunge. Fifth grade was Three Days Grace, which is angry punkness, but nothing that crazy. Then, somehow, I got to Korn and Five Finger Death Punch a few years later, to which I still cannot make sense of. That eventually evolved into my favorite band, Soundgarden, and then to what it is now.

What is it now? More heaviness, featuring bands like Tool and

Pantera. These bands in particular have great songs like "Prison Sex," "Piss" and "Good Friend and a Bottle of Pills."

So uh, yeah.

This deep love for heavy also evolved into just about the darkest wardrobe selection I could ever strive for, as it seems that these bands exclusively produce black shirts.

The heaviness has also contributed a great deal to my mood, as typical music is too bland and upbeat for me now. Blaring songs like "Piss" on repeat during quarantine has begun to destroy my near-perfect hearing and my complete view on everything around me.

I've experienced three of the five total angriest moments of my life just in the past seven months. Whether it was shouting so much my voice was gone for several days or a lot of pillow punching, rage is all too familiar in my life.

During a lot of my time home, I viewed the world with anger. But never that feeling of empathy I probably should have.

I ended two friendships over the summer. Due to the added time alone with myself, I developed the sense of being finished with people's bullshit. These two former friends truly got on my final nerves, and I've moved on.

The insurmountable feelings of rage have mostly disappeared now, but lord do I still get mad every now and then.

Moral of the story, heavy music is probably contributing to your constant anger and very different world view, but you shouldn't try to change it.

Why?

Because it's goddamn electric!

Something, no, *someone* on the horizon

Here we are with probably the finale.

Not of COVID, but just this writing.

Man, I wish it included COVID's end as well.

A lot has happened since March. The sudden surprise of the virus has ruined honestly, everything.

I experienced months of depression that I combated with anger and rage. I came back to campus for this semester, and it has been rocky. I thought that depression had disappeared, but it's only heightened. This last month has been the hardest month of my entire life.

A lot of things kept going wrong and I felt like giving up.

But there's something on the horizon.

Or should I say, someone.

I've met someone I would love to spend the rest of my life with.

She's genuinely all I've got going for me.

And it's so welcomed. All I want is for things to work out.

Within the next month, the semester will be over and we'll have winter break for two months. I'm not sure if this is the beginning of the end, or the end of the beginning.

I'm so lost, but at the same time, I'm not.

My life seems to fluctuate so very much for unknown reasons. Sometimes I feel like I'm drowning. Sometimes I feel high and dry. It's a never-ending cycle.

But I need to look on the bright side, that being the future. I'm becoming happy again and it can only go up from here.

This year has been shit, but everything seems to be nicely shaping up for 2021. Anything is better than this.

CHAPTER 17

Adam Osha

This marked the third class in which I have had Adam as a student and his writing talent just continues to elevate. He was blunt and conversational about bad habits, about wanting to do better, about a needed getaway to party with friends and about the power of hobbies to free the mind.

I needed to change

It was a month into quarantine, and I had formed some nasty habits. No longer bound by the routine of school, I had no structure. The only good thing I was doing for myself was work, and I didn't love that. But with nothing else going on, work seemed a welcome break in the day.

Every day was the same mundane routine.

Wake up, rip the bong, go back to sleep, wake up, eat food, begin my day.

At first, I thought quarantine would give me a needed reprieve from the stress of student life, but that didn't turn out to be true. My bad habits during quarantine only got worse, and the motivation to do anything disappeared.

I was stoned or tired all the time. My diet was trash, I didn't exercise, I slept past noon every day.

How could I possibly care about school in the comfort of my own home? I thought I was very fortunate some days to not have any classes where I had to be present for Zoom calls, but that also led me to become a little careless and forgetful about school.

Because I live in a small town with not many friends nearby, I missed everyone from school. Most of my college friends lived more than an hour away, and I had no idea when I would see them again. Everyone was super paranoid about this virus.

At the beginning of the pandemic, I played the victim card big time, just living in a lot of negativity because that was all I was surrounded by.

I was sad about things in my personal life, and I was sad about the state that our world was in.

This pandemic reminds me that we cannot control every aspect of our lives, but we can control how we react. We have to consciously make efforts to replace the negative with positive. It's a lot harder to be positive, especially during this time. But there are things you can do to help yourself.

Every so often, I have an experience that allows me to get a fresh start mentally and helps me switch my perspective.

I knew I had to break this pattern and create a new one. I needed some sort of routine to help me regain structure in my life, so I quit smoking throughout the day, which changed a lot for me.

I had a lot more energy and was motivated to do more.

I took up some new hobbies I'd never made time for, but have always wanted to try, and made an effort to eliminate or decrease my bad habits.

I'm reminded that when I am productive, I feel good about myself.

Every day I continue to search for balance in my life; it's the only way to stay in line. No matter how stuck you feel, try to think about the areas in which you are doing too much or too little of something, and that can apply to anything.

Do things that make you happy, and never become too comfortable with where you're at. One change leads to a series of changes.

Focusing on me

I needed some new hobbies.

What to do? I contemplated.

What are people supposed to do? Like ever.

Life seems pretty simple. You go to school, go to college, get a job, pay bills, get married, have some kids, and then retire.

It's not that simple, especially to someone who can't accept that.

I won't accept that; it sounds awful.

Which brings me back to the question of: What are people supposed to do?

Our lives revolve around getting money, but what if they didn't?

This pandemic put a lot of people out of work. And while there was a lot of uncertainty and fear, there was also free time. A window of opportunity.

When living in fear of the unknown, it can be difficult to do anything.

Creativity may not have been at the forefront of everyone's mind, but it was for me. It always is.

I feel trapped by school and work, like I'm being held back from what I truly want to do. There is never any free time, and if there is, it gets spent just tripping about schoolwork that needs to get done. But with that feeling comes the urge to escape and create.

It's like I can't put all my energy into something when there are many other things consuming my thoughts and emotions.

This pandemic changed that for me though. I stopped looking at the news; I truly believe they push out negativity to keep people scared.

While there are very real things going on in our world right now, I decided to not let that consume me. I will not overthink things I cannot control.

It's tough. You don't want to be completely oblivious, but you don't want that to be all you think about.

As far as I'm concerned, all that shit's fake.

It's not, but maybe if I pretend, I won't be so anxious.

It's almost as if we were created to create. Use that to free your mind.

Focus on the things you can control, let go of what you can't. Immerse yourself in what feels good.

I'm going to choose to focus on my life and what is real to me. I am tuning into myself and tuning out the rest of the world.

I will continue to enjoy my new hobbies: playing bass, making clothes and art, and tending to my cannabis plants. That makes me happy.

I will end with a quote by the late Terence McKenna: "Art, sculpture, poetry, painting, dance is like the footprints of where the imagination has been."

It went too fast

It had been about three months since I'd seen any of my friends. Between the lockdown and the distance between us, it hadn't been easy.

You really want to see people.

Humans need that. But you think about the what-ifs. We're in Vermont, it's probably safe, but *what if?*

What if I got my family sick? Grandparents specifically. I know that was at the front of most people's minds as well.

People were still partying, and it looked fun. I wanted to; I missed having fun. But what if I went to a gathering that led to an outbreak?

No good. The risks outweighed one night.

But my friends and I wanted to party. There had to be a way we could make something work.

That's when we thought of renting an Airbnb for a few nights with some friends.

A small group, everyone would quarantine before, or agree to try their best not go anywhere unnecessary.

We originally were thinking of around 10 people or so, but it turned out to be five, which was probably for the better.

We found something affordable and semi-discreet; we didn't want to annoy any neighbors by our shenanigans.

We drove through what seemed to be the middle of nowhere until we arrived at a small cabin in Stratton, Vermont.

It was a little log cabin with a red roof. It seemed pretty tiny, but it supposedly slept eight.

You know those places that just look small on the outside? It was like that; the inside seemed to be another world.

"No way all these rooms fit in this little cabin," I thought.

The first words spoken as we walked in were, "Damn this is chill I would actually live here."

Everyone agreed. It would be our home for the next three nights.

We all sat at the table and caught up on everything. The sound of beers cracking circled around the table like dominoes.

And just like that, the blur of a weekend went by and I wasn't sure when I'd see them again.

CHAPTER 18

Aris Sherwood

Aris is one of the editors of the student newspaper and has a very natural, conversational storytelling voice. In true chronological fashion, which she planned from the start, Aris weaved tales of lost firsts and lost goodbyes but also triumphs, including her sister's scaled-down wedding that was perfect.

It was only the start

It was almost apocalyptic.

The posters that hung around the nearly empty campus are what scared me the most. The warning signs and how to prevent COVID-19 followed me through the buildings, through the halls, stared at me while I sat in the Campus Center, with the echoes of students who sat here days prior in this now-abandoned room.

These posters foreshadowed a new normal none of us saw coming. For weeks, I thought about those posters. I wondered if they were still up. I wondered how long they were going to be there. The students who flooded my beloved campus, now only memories. With only a poster to prove we were once there.

In the beginning, we didn't know what was happening. Yes, about the virus – the rapidly spreading illness that would inevitably hit our state.

It was unknown, unheard of.

We didn't know what to make of it.

But the feeling of uncertainty I had when I sat in the dance studio that fateful day still haunts me.

My trip to New York had been canceled. I was upset, understandably. I had been looking forward to this trip for months. And at the time, I had yet to know about the severity of the virus.

So I had gone to school the next day, wearing a mask as I had come down with a cold and my mother was worried sick.

I took it off later as I felt self-conscious. No one around me was wearing a mask.

The timeline of the following events is foggy. But at some point, we learned that campus would be shutting down.

My heart shattered. I lived at home already, but campus was the place where I felt the most myself. My happiest was when I was walking from Leavenworth to the dance studio, a Coffee Cottage bagel in hand. And I had to say goodbye.

The theater department gathered in the dance studio. We talked about our feelings, our worries. We all shared the same grief.

As I said goodbye to my friends, I kept telling myself that it would only be two weeks. I'll see these faces in two weeks.

But this apocalypse wouldn't end in two weeks.

No, it was just getting started.

I would have done things differently, had I known

I wish I could remember March.

But the truth is, I don't.

March has become a blur, a faded memory that lives in the back of my mind.

I think I felt so many feelings during that time: confusion, relief, sadness, anger.

This was still the early stages of quarantine, still the beginning of COVID-19. I was still getting used to online classes, almost happy that my new schedule allowed me to sleep more, almost whenever I wanted.

But I hated seeing my friends through the screen.

Just weeks before, I was in the dance studio, holding on to the bar while Maya adjusted my turnout, cracking jokes with Daniel in between combos.

Just weeks before, I was sitting in *The Spartan* student newspaper office with Jay and Caton, yelling about whether Ariana Grande should've won album of the year and complaining about our newest stories.

My favorite people and my favorite moments were now behind a computer screen, in tiny boxes. And here I was, boxed in my own room, trying to find the normalcy in this seemingly un-normal circumstance.

I could still fix my own turnout while holding onto a chair in my room. I could still hear Jay reassuring me that he could in fact "hear me" (inside joke from a classmate who would always say "I hear ya").

But it wasn't the same.

I think at this point we knew we would not be going back to campus for a while. And it took me a while to be OK with it. I didn't really have a choice but to be OK with it.

One July day, I was talking to my friend, Jordan. We had weirdly gotten closer in our distances than when we were in the dance studio together, but we have always been good friends. We were talking about our memories together.

Jordan, at this point, had graduated, and I'll never be able to see her in the dance studio again, whenever we do go back.

I remember telling her I wish I savored our moments together. If I had known our hello that fateful day would've been our last, I would've held on to it just a little bit longer. If I had known our hug goodbye would have been our last hug, I would've held on just a little tighter.

Some of my closest friends have graduated, and I'll never be able to see them the same way again. I never got closure from that. And I wish, more than anything, I could go back and live in those moments just one more time.

Even my friends who haven't graduated yet. I haven't seen Daniel, my best friend, in six months. I would give anything to be in his warm, comforting embrace again.

I would give anything to be in Maya's office, talking to her about everything yet nothing at the same time.

I would give anything to be in *The Spartan* office again, the room so tiny that all of our knees could be touching, all there connected by one thing.

And in March, I looked at these people I love more than anything through a computer screen. They were right in front of me, but so far away.

Sick of living a metaphor

Does anyone remember April?

I'm seriously asking. Looking back, it feels like April didn't even exist. Like I closed my eyes one March day, and opened them to find myself here, writing this in September.

According to my faded memories and social media footprint, I apparently was doing whatever I could to distract myself and not be so bored all of the time.

April 9, I started listening to a Greek mythology audiobook that has since been abandoned.

April 12, I redid my entire room, which was a pretty common narrative for a lot of young women in quarantine.

April 13, I re-created my mom's senior photo.

April 17, my story about my favorite high school teacher was first published in *The Rutland Herald*.

April 25, my editorial on racism in my city's school was published.

April 25 again, my niece and sister flew down for a visit.

Here is living, physical proof that I existed during the month of April, but why does it feel like April was another life?

I wish I could find a profound answer to this question. I wish I could write a poetic response to this prompt.

But the truth is, the time we are living in is really shitty. And different. We are stuck in our rooms all day expected to carry on with a bit of normalcy. It's no wonder the days get blurred together.

And it's all meaningless.

Remember that time when we thought quarantine would be a chance for self-improvement? You download a book about Greek mythology thinking you're gonna be the world's expert on Persephone only to give up not even a quarter into it because you have a hard time understanding. And it's all just one stupid metaphor.

I don't think I wanna live in a metaphor anymore.

I wanna exist again.

Pandemic gift came in small packages

In May, school ended.

I had slowly but surely gotten used to online Zoom University, but before I knew it, it was over. I had somehow passed all of my classes and even ended the semester with the best grades I've ever had.

I was really surprised by this; I honestly thought I was gonna flunk out of all my classes.

So now I was in my room, where I had been for months.

And I needed a job.

Badly.

Desperately.

I worked at a school before, and with virtual learning and social distancing, that was out of the question.

And so was summer camp, which I had been looking forward to for months.

So I needed a job.

Here's the thing about me: I'm really bad at working. The one time I had a retail job, I had to quit after six days. I've been lucky for years to have worked at the same place, but now, here I was, applying to every chain business in town. I was hoping to score a job but secretly praying I wouldn't hear back at the same time.

Then, one day, I got a message from a mom of kids I worked with before.

"Hi Aris, I am Landon and Sara's mother. I was wondering if you would come to our house on Tuesdays and Thursdays to watch the kids? Let me know if you are interested. We hope you are well!"

I immediately jumped at the opportunity.

Finally, a job!

But little did I know that baby-sitting Landon and Sara would be so much more than a job.

They had another baby sitter who wasn't able to watch them on Tuesdays and Thursdays anymore, which lucky for me, meant I watched them on those days while they still had virtual school and their parents worked.

Then, it led into the summer. I helped watch them from May straight through August. And when they found out they would be doing virtual school on Wednesdays, they asked me if I could watch them then too.

I know it seems silly to be thankful for two little kids you get paid to watch, but I really am.

They came to me at just the right time.

I had spent months being alone in my room. I hadn't seen my best friends since March. But seeing those little nerds reminds me what it's like to be loved by other people. To socialize, to chat about our days and do silly things with.

It was almost a bit of normal, and even though there are days when I'm annoyed at them or when they say something mean to me, we still sit together and eat chicken nuggets while watching "Mr. Beast."

And that is something.

I love taking care of them, and even if they won't admit it, I think they like having me there too.

A perfect wedding in spite of it all

In June, my sister got married. Since she was 15, she had been planning her wedding to a T.

And, when her dream became a reality, it was almost perfect.

Almost.

Her original wedding had been planned for June 20, 2020. The venue was set, the dress was fitted, the invites were sent.

But then, the pandemic hit, and the moment she had been dreaming of for years had come crashing down.

But like most pandemic weddings, they decided to elope, with a small group of people, in our backyard.

And, it was perfect.

My mom set up the most beautiful archway, and decorated it with lace and flowers that had been planted one year ago. The weather was amazing, and it was just my family and her husband's family, a beautiful Vermont June and it was perfect.

No, it wasn't ideal.

It wasn't what we had planned. But we made do, and we made beautiful memories in the midst of hardship.

And I think that's the biggest takeaway I've learned since the beginning of the pandemic. You can plan and plan, you can have your future and your goals all drawn up, but before you know it, changes can happen that halt everything.

But what's important is how you deal with it, and what you do about it. In the beginning, we were all scared.

Of course we're still scared and we're sad at this tragic moment in history. But we've proven we can overcome in the eyes of tragedy, and still create beautiful memories.

Safely, of course.

We have been forced to adapt to these unfortunate circumstances. Some, more than others. But there can still be beautiful moments, as long as you remember to cherish your loved ones and find beauty in the unknown.

When my niece and nephew get older, I hope my sister tells them of the pandemic wedding and how strong it made us.

Afterword

NOW THAT YOU have finished this roller-coaster ride of stories from students who are trying desperately for normalcy in these unchartered pandemic waters, I hope you better understand their plight.

I hope when you interact with young adults, you have a new-found perspective of what they are up against and all the things they sacrificed because of COVID-19.

But I also hope they inspired you – like they did me.

I hope you see our college students as talented, intelligent, thoughtful and – albeit battered and beaten down – resilient.

I said in the dedication at the beginning of this book that I basically compiled their work and published it because I believe it's a small win for them in a time when wins are hard to come by.

And, my hope is to create a scholarship from proceeds to help reward them and future students.

Another little win, perhaps.

David Blow

DAVID BLOW is in his 16th year as a professor of Media and Communication at Castleton University, a second career for the award-winning journalist from Queensbury, New York.

After 15 years as a reporter and editor at *The Post-Star* newspaper in Glens Falls, New York, he traded the newsroom for the classroom at his alma mater, completing a full-circle journey inspired by Terry Dalton, his former professor at Castleton.

In 2013, Blow published his first book, "Blow by Blow: A Quarter-Century of Voices from My Notebook," detailing highlights of his writing career, including a bizarre murder and a Robert Redford interview.

His byline can still frequently be found on feature stories and columns for *The Post-Star*, proving what he tells his students: he sees story ideas everywhere and can't turn it off.

He loves teaching and feeds off the energy of students when they score their first byline – or when they get excited about a project like "COVID Chronicles."

He is married with two daughters and, in his spare time, loves to ski, skate, ride his bike, travel, listen to live music and enjoy summer-time poolside with family and friends.

CPSIA information can be obtained
at www.ICGtesting.com
Printed in the USA
FSHW020620240421

9 781977 239150